ONE YOUNG MAN'S WAR

(1939–1946)

All profits from the sale of this book will go to the Welfare Fund of the Coastal Forces Veterans' Association.

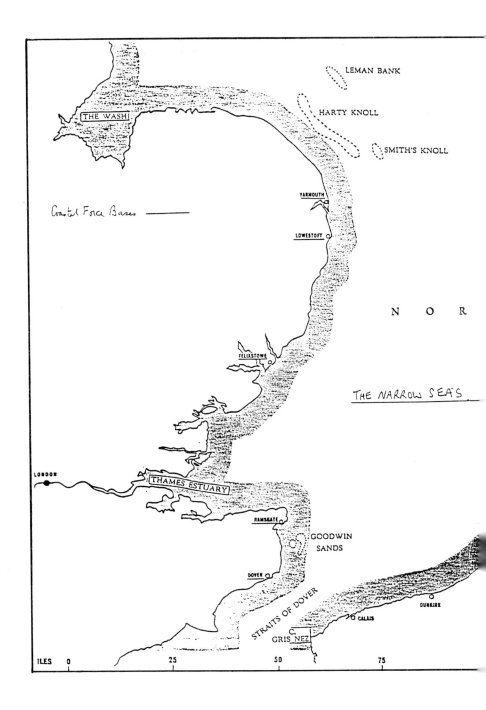

LEMAN BANK

HARTY KNOLL

SMITH'S KNOLL

THE WASH

Coastal Force Bases ————

YARMOUTH

LOWESTOFT

N O R

FELIXSTOWE

THE NARROW SEA'S

LONDON

THAMES ESTUARY

RAMSGATE

GOODWIN SANDS

DOVER

STRAITS OF DOVER

DUNKIRK

CALAIS

C. GRIS NEZ

MILES 0   25   50   75

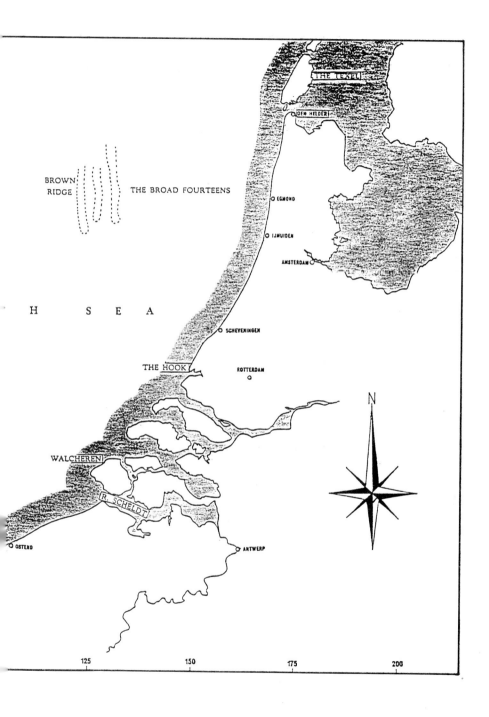

BROWN
RIDGE

THE BROAD FOURTEENS

THE TEXEL

DEN HELDER

EGMOND

IJMUIDEN

AMSTERDAM

H   S   E   A

SCHEVENINGEN

THE HOOK

ROTTERDAM

WALCHEREN

R. SCHELDT

OSTEND

ANTWERP

N

125   150   175   200

Drawing of author in 1989, by Donald Romeo

ONE YOUNG MAN'S WAR
(1939–1946)

Michael Bray

A Square One Publication

First published in 1993 by
Square One Publications
Saga House, Sansome Place, Worcester WR1 1UA

©Francis Arthur Michael Bray 1993
ISBN: 1 872017 60 6

British Library Cataloguing-in-Publication Data.
A catalogue record for this book is available from the
British Library.

*Photographs mainly by Author
Portrait drawing of Lt. P. G. Lee by Peter Scott*

Typeset by Avon Dataset Ltd, Bidford on Avon, Warwickshire
Printed by Antony Rowe Ltd.

CONTENTS

ACKNOWLEDGEMENTS

I have to thank Lady Scott for permission to use extracts and illustrations from "The Battle of the Narrow Seas" by her late husband, Lieut. Commander Sir Peter Scott, CH, CBE, DSC and Bar, RNVR, and to Michael Russell (Publishing) Ltd, for permission to quote extracts from Sir John Colville's "Footprints in Time".

I could never have completed this book without the tireless help of Mrs Suzie Quinn, who typed my tapes with great accuracy, from a distance of thousands of miles, and for the forbearance and encouragement given to me by my wife, Paula, during the birth of the book. I owe them both a great deal.

FOREWORD

by Commander Christopher Dreyer DSO DSC RN ret'd

I suppose that Michael Bray was a fair example of the fine type of young man who found his way into Coastal Forces in the last War, and became the Commanding Officer of a Motor Gunboat at the age of 20. Now, at 71, he has written down some of his memories, largely of his time in Dickie Richards' flotilla of MGBs in Ramsgate and also, for the last 2 years of the war, in a Fleet destroyer, HMS *Undaunted*, in the Home Fleet and the Pacific – Russian convoys, the invasion of France and then the British Pacific Fleet.

He intersperses his story with extracts from his letters to his parents and also, very appropriately, with pieces from Peter Scott's "Battle of the Narrow Seas", and these help very well to tie the whole memorable narrative together. Since I was the Senior Officer MTBs in Dover for some of the time that Michael Bray was commanding an MGB in Ramsgate, and since Dickie Richards was a great friend of mine, much of the story of that time is very clear to me and I well remember many of the incidents.

Although a young man reading the story today might be tempted to think what fun it all was and how satisfying a life it must have been – and to an extent it was both those things – I believe that he would be brought down to earth again, quite quickly, by the realisation that a tragically large number of excellent young men – officers and ratings – lost their lives in those jolly times. It was fun and it was indeed sometimes satisfying, but it was also lethal. War is always a disaster.

I am honoured now to be the President of our survivors club – the Coastal Forces Veterans' Association. We, who had the good fortune not to be killed, are constantly aware of our wartime shipmates, who didn't have our luck. At all our meetings, reunions and memorials we take a special pride in remembering them and in recognising the tragedy of their cut-off lives.

This book will be a valuable addition to the growing list of reminiscences about time in Coastal Forces in the 1939–45 War, and I commend it warmly to anyone who has an interest in those boats, with which all of us who were involved in or with them, maintain a permanent love-hate relationship, and, fortunately for us, a tendency to remember only the good times.

PREFACE

The events remembered and described in this book took place either side of 50 years ago and if my memory has let me down on some incidents, then I apologise.

I write from the balcony of our Caribbean house, looking across the startlingly blue sea to the island of Nevis, and the wreath of white clouds around the summit of its volcano.

It was in the late 18th Century that Admiral Nelson and his band of brothers sailed and fought these waters. He was married in Nevis, protected his fleet in the hurricane season at English Harbour in Antigua to the S.E. of us, and it was off Guadeloupe, 50 miles to the south, that Admiral Rodney defeated the French fleet at the battle of the Saints.

This island was seized from the British by the French in 1782, and some of the french guns still lie on St George's Hill.

Everywhere, if you seek it, is the ghost of the British Navy of that day.

Our war in small boats in the narrow seas of the English Channel was not unlike that of Nelson's days. We were also a "band of brothers", we fought our enemy at very close quarters, almost hand to hand at times, and we developed a camaraderie amongst ourselves that has lasted to the present day.

Admiral Nelson prayed on the eve of the Battle of Trafalgar, "May the great God whom I worship, grant to my Country, and for the benefit of Europe in general, a great and glorious victory, and may no misconduct in anyone tarnish it . . ."

As you will read in this book, I and many others were guilty of numerous "misconducts" during our time in the Navy, but I like to think that Admiral Nelson would have understood, and turned a blind eye to them, and not considered that they, in any way, "tarnished the great and glorious victory" that the Allies eventually achieved in 1945, and to which many of my friends and colleagues gave their lives.

This book is dedicated to their memory.

Michael Bray
Montserrat, W. Indies
March 1992

CHAPTER 1

Ordinary Seaman

I was 18 in April 1939 and left school in July. It was intended that I should go up to Cambridge in the autumn and during the summer holidays I was sent to live with a family in Brittany to improve my French. This was fun but I learnt little French, as there were two English girls staying there, and we spent most of the time on the beach.

For the last 12 months it had been obvious that war with Germany was likely to break out, it was just a question of time, and during my last few terms at Charterhouse we had been put on to digging trenches in case of air raids. By mid-August things looked very bad so I decided to go home from France, and war was finally declared on 3rd September.

When the first air raid warning was sounded that morning of 3rd September my father started a routine of filling a bath with water and putting a large mattress over the drawing room window. Needless to say he soon gave this up after a few false alarms.

My father was born in 1880, at the height of Victorian prosperity and power. He was educated at Charterhouse School and Heidelberg University.

His family had had a long connection with the silk trade, and lived around Spitalfields in the centre of London, since the 17th Century, but his grandfather qualified as a doctor, and his father worked in the City of London, as an Insurance Broker at Lloyd's of London, and around 1870, formed his own company, where my father joined him in about 1900.

My mother's family were French Huguenots, who had left Burgundy in about 1699, and settled in England. They married into English families and prospered, while their sons entered the Army and the Church, as was their wont in those days.

My father and mother had seven children, of whom I was the sixth.

My brothers and brothers-in-law joined the regular Army, the Church, the City, the regular Navy, and the wartime RAF.

All my brothers, and my youngest sister, went up to Cambridge University.

That was my family background.

Having left school I felt restless and didn't particularly want to go up to Cambridge now that we were at war, so eventually, under the influence of a friend, Joe Lowe, I went up to London and joined the Royal Naval Volunteer Reserve (RNVR) at HMS *President* on the Thames Embankment as an ordinary seaman, and was told that I would shortly be mobilised. I joined the Navy because at school we were always hearing from the Masters terrible stories about mud, barbed wire, and trenches in France, so I vowed never to join the Army.

Naturally my mother and father were very disappointed that I was not going to Cambridge and as call-up was then at the age of 20, it was quite unnecessary for me to go when I was only 18. However they were very good and did not try and influence me, and eventually in about October I received my calling-up papers, reported to HMS *President*, and was sent up to Skegness, where Butlins Holiday Camp had been commandeered and turned into a training base.

I spent about a month there, living two to a hut, learning seamanship and taking part in endless drilling, and being employed in filling sandbags on the beach so that the

Two Naval Brothers-in-Law. Cdr John Meares RN (later OBE, DSC
RN retd.) and Ordinary Seaman M. Bray RNVR

buildings could be protected from bombs.

From there I was sent to Devonport Barracks for a few weeks, and then to a destroyer, HMS *Electra*, which was engaged on Atlantic convoy work.

This was reality with a capital R. Living on a crowded and uncomfortable messdeck with people from a very different background to my own, sleeping in a hammock, and suffering from seasickness, the excitement of going to war very quickly faded away. However I was earning 2 shillings a day which was the first money that I had ever earned!

Towards the end of the year I volunteered to be trained as an ASDIC rating, which was the anti-submarine arm of the Navy and involved being sent to a special training school, HMS *Osprey*, at Portland for a three months' course. ASDIC stood for Anti-Submarine Detection Investigation Committee and the British Navy had developed a very efficient system which was based on the transmission of a sonic pulse under water which was reflected back by any large mass such as a submarine or a shoal of fish.

A well-trained operator could tell the difference, because the transmissions were on a very narrow beam and therefore he could tell the size of the object by the number of degrees that the echo covered. He could also tell the distance away by the time taken for the echo to return and also whether the object was moving away or towards, by the "doppler effect", which was the difference in pitch between the transmission and the echo back. If the submarine was going away the returning echo would be at a lower pitch. The operator was therefore able to tell the bridge, when he had a good contact, that it appeared to be a submarine and it was moving either left or right, coming towards or going away, and it was at a distance of so many yards. He could also give the bridge the compass bearing of the echo.

The maximum range was about one mile, and the ship would alter course towards the contact, being kept advised by the operator of any change of course of the target, and eventually would be able to fire a pattern of depth charges over the submarine which stood a good chance of being damaged or sunk.

On our three months' course we had a very detailed training on the technical side and also plenty of practice, as a submarine was attached to the base, and we had the large motor yacht *Shemara*, fitted with ASDIC, and in Portland Bay we could hunt the submarine, and really get to know what it sounded like. Apart from the "ping" we could also hear its propellers at short range.

I found the course very interesting, I had a good ear and I soon became quite proficient. The *Shemara* was owned by Sir Bernard Docker, the Chairman of Daimlers, and

4

was a very fine yacht. He took her back after the War. We were told a story that the Captain used the owner's cabin, which was full of gadgets, and one day, lying in his berth, he pressed one of many buttons, and the partition beside his berth dropped away electrically, and he found himself alongside the first lieutenant in his berth!

The Naval Base at Portland was protected from attack by enemy shipping, either surface or submarine, by what was called a "Loop". This was a long loop of wire laid right across the bay on the bottom of the sea, and any ship crossing it would set up an electrical current and therefore give its presence away. The wires from the loop came ashore at the ASDIC base, and one unpleasant duty that we had to perform was to stand guard over the place on the beach where the wires came ashore.

This meant that we had to take turns to go on sentry duty during the night, with a rifle and bayonet, and I can still remember the awfulness of being alone in the middle of a dark night, standing on the beach, wondering whether a German raiding party was going to land to cut the wires and murder the sentry. Some of the most miserable and lonely hours of my life were spent standing there in the winter cold and wet, on what seemed an endless four hour watch.

Eventually I qualified, had the ASDIC operator badge sewn onto my uniform, and was appointed as an operator to HMS *Wild Swan*, an old destroyer built in the First War.

She was based at Devonport and engaged on Atlantic convoy work.

By this time I had got over my seasickness, and at least it was warm in the ASDIC cabinet which was at the bottom of the ship, but which would not have been a good place if we had been bombed or torpedoed.

When we were on watch we would operate the set for half an hour at a time and then change over for a rest, and we had to sweep the sea from 90 degrees on the beam

Wild Swan

through ahead to 90 degrees on the other beam in 5 degree steps. With earphones on, one heard the "ping" of the transmission every 30 seconds or so which became rather monotonous, unless one received an answering "ping" back again.

One was then electrified, and after satisfying oneself that it really was an echo one alerted the bridge, and then set out to find whether the object was moving and if so in which direction and whether or not it changed course, or whether it behaved like a shoal of fish.

These were very exciting moments and obviously rather rare, but on these convoys we did get some good contacts, carried out attacks, and in the opinion of the Captain we made one or more "kills".

Otherwise convoy work was very boring, and uncomfortable when the weather was bad, but one got into a routine of 4 hours on duty and 8 hours off throughout the 24 hours of the day, and I was able to read a lot.

In about March or April 1940, the ship was ordered up to Dover together with the other destroyers in our Flotilla. I

6

can't remember what we did there but it was a nice change from convoy work and we spent quite a lot of time in Harbour, and I started taking navigation lessons from the Navigator.

He encouraged me to apply for a commission, and in due course my papers were sent forward to the Admiralty with a recommendation from the Captain.

September 1939 to May 1940, apart from the war at sea, was known as the "phoney war" as nothing much happened and the Allied armies faced each other behind their respective defensive lines, in the case of the Allies, the Maginot Line, and for the Germans, the Siegfried Line.

However all this changed dramatically on 10th May 1940 when the German Blitzkrieg against the Low Countries started without warning, and the German Army swept into Holland and Belgium and occupied them in a matter of days.

On that day, 10th May 1940, we were ordered to proceed to Holland, with an army unit on board which was to be landed, and amongst other things we were ordered to try and find the Dutch Royal Family and bring them back to England.

It was an amazing change as, with our armed soldiers on board, we steamed at full speed towards The Hook of Holland, the entrance to the River Maas, and the first thing we saw on arrival was a Dutch troopship being bombed and sunk, from which we picked up some survivors, and then proceeded up the river.

It was a beautiful sight with the bulb fields in full bloom on either side, but ugly with Junkers 52 aircraft coming in low and dropping sticks of parachutists into those bulb fields, and it was difficult to believe that it was real. But it was.

As soon as we had gone up the river, German aircaft came in and dropped mines at the entrance of the river so that we were bottled up for the time being.

Taking troops to Hook of Holland, May 10th 1940 on board
HMS *Wild Swan*

Next stop Holland, and the War

Picking up survivors
from bombed
troopship off Dutch
Coast — May 10th
1940

On the dockside at
Hook of Holland
Troops disembarking
from
HMS *Wild Swan* —
May 10th 1940

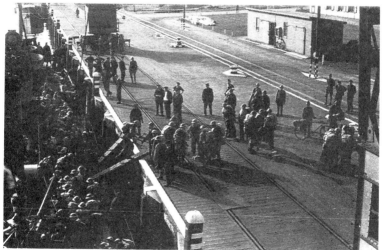

We didn't find the Dutch Royal Family, and at night we had to tie up to the river bank, but because of the danger from German parachutists we had to post sentries from the ship's crew on the river bank. We were told that some Germans were disguised as Nuns, but that you could tell them from Nuns by their boots! The troops that we had brought over had gone ashore and I don't know where they went or whatever happened to them.

We were subject to bombing and also attack from the shore and it was a very uncomfortable period.

I had always been very interested in aircraft (my father had been in the Royal Flying Corps in the First World War), and I could distinguish between British and German planes and so knew which were friendly and which were hostile.

On hearing this the Captain ordered me up on to the bridge to help spot aircraft in case we were attacked, which was of course very flattering for me.

As the German army swiftly moved forward, our position became untenable, and the mines in the entrance to the river having been swept, we left Holland and set off for Chatham Dockyard for an overdue refit.

I have recently found two letters that I wrote to my parents at the time, describing life on the lower deck of HMS *Wild Swan*.

                                        Mess 5
                                        Wild Swan
                                        c/o G.P.O.
4.3.40

Dearest Ma and Pa
    As I write we are on our way to Dover with a convoy. We ought to be back in Devonport by next Monday (the 11th). Except for today the weather has been awful.
    Out in the Atlantic, we rolled right over on our beam ends for days on end, and waves swept over the decks.
    I felt very miserable, as I was ill most of the time, and

we were working in two watches, 4 hours on and 4 off, night and day. There was chaos on our messdeck, water, corpses, plates, pots and pans swinging from one side to the other. Even the mess tables came adrift.

We lost our wretched 'Middie' overboard. Poor lad, he went to call the Sub-Lieut and on the way back, must have been swept away.

Today has been lovely just like summer.

We have had quite a good convoy, 54 ships and they look lovely today, steaming along on a calm sea in the sun.

Tues. Since I wrote this, we have left our convoy, and gone chasing a sub. We got the message saying there was one loafing at about 8 o'clock in the evening and dashed off back into the Atlantic.

We contacted at about 11 and laid our "eggs" An enormous patch of oil appeared in the searchlight, and lots of bubbles. Conditions were perfect, and it was a lovely night. There was another destroyer there and she looked very pretty, tearing through the water with a phosphorescent glow streaming from her bows, and her searchlight playing on the water where her charges were exploding.

It was very hard work and I was closed up in the ASDIC cabinet till 3.40 a.m. I got into my hammock for about 2 hours, but then the target was detected to be moving slowly, so in we went again to drop more "charges". She hasn't moved since (it is 7 p.m.) and we will wait a little longer, and then we know she is done for.

The depth is 71 fathoms and the bottom is flat with no wrecks, so she can't be hiding. She sounds as if she is breaking up.

Altogether about 30 charges were dropped. The other destroyer left us to watch over the sub, and before she left she signalled "Congratulations *Wild Swan*, a good job well done".

Tomorrow we will be back home, excused our convoy.

Wed. Last night about 8 we got another SOS, a sub had been sighted, and so off we went full belt again.

We got a contact at midnight and proceeded to drop charges everywhere, and stayed there all night watching the target.

We later got a message from the Admiralty, saying that our first was a sub, and our second a new wreck. (All the things in this letter are confidential)

On the way back home, we thought we had another sub, and dropped a charge. It was a shoal of cod, and we stopped the ship and picked up about 130 averaging 15−20 lbs each. It was a wonderful sight; hundreds of buckets, fishing nets, boat hooks and other strange fishing implements appeared, and tremendous efforts were made to get in the fish.

Greed was the undoing of several people, including the Gunners Mate, a very pompous personnage, who disappeared head first overboard.

One bright person produced a large tin hip bath, threw it overboard and jumped in. It was alright until, full of fish, it was filled by a wave and both sank. Having hauled in the fish and the too eager fishermen, we moved off.

The fish were very good when we had them for supper (as also did most other ships moored near us).

I must stop now.

Your loving son
Michael

P.S. When we were cruising over our first sub in the afternoon of that day, there was suddenly a tremendous internal explosion, so there can be no doubt that she was destroyed.

5 Mess
Wild Swan
c/o G.P.O.

11.5.40

My dearest Mummy and Daddy

It was marvellous seeing you on Wednesday, thank you so much for coming down to Dover.

May 10th 1940. Destroyers of the Dover Patrol steaming at full
speed to Holland

Well, things have been happening so quickly, that I can
hardly follow them.

As I suspected, when the blow on Holland fell, we, the
Dover Patrol, had to do the initial operations.

The news had hardly come through before we were
loading extra supplies of ammunition, bren guns, anti-
tank rifles, and just over a hundred troops with tons of
T.N.T., a small B.E.F. whose job it was to delay the
German advance by cutting communications. Nobody
knew where we were going, but it was expected to be
pretty suicidal, so all confidential books were landed, and
demolition charges were placed on all secret instruments.
By noon everything was ready, and we all left for
different destinations, Battle Ensigns flying proudly from
all available halyards.

It was a grand sight the whole flotilla going full out,
racing thru' the lines of ships in the Downs. From
messages we received we learnt the coast was mined, and
the Germans were already there (we were going to the
mouth of the River Maas and landing our troops at the
Hook of Holland). I was on the bridge, as neither Jimmy

13

nor the skipper were good at distinguishing between friendly and enemy planes.

Luckily the Germans hadn't quite got there when we arrived, and we met a pilot boat. The skipper said thru' the mike, "Good Afternoon Captain. This is H.M.S. *Wild Swan*. I have been ordered to land troops on the railway jetty, and give you any help you want." As we came alongside the jetty the Dutch soldiers and sailors and civilians were shouting, "Three cheers for England".

The Germans seemed to have free use of the sky, and they didn't seem to take much notice of us. One, as a friendly gesture, dumped four bombs about 300 yards ahead of us which demolished a warehouse. We returned the compliment with everything we had, which made him suddenly remember he had an urgent date elsewhere.

13.5.40. Back at Dover. Will continue the narrative. The Germans were pretty near and we could hear rifle and machine gun fire all night, about a mile away. The Airport at Rotterdam was ablaze and lit up the sky with a great red glow. The other side of the river a battery of guns was shelling a wood on our side, and the shells sounded like express trains, as they went overhead. Also that evening a Commander and four volunteer ratings who had taken passage with us, went on up the river in a small steamer, to blow up something, unfortunately they went up on a magnetic mine. He looked a very nice man.

The Germans had been landing troops by parachute all night and they were hiding in a wood near the river bank, so the next day, we went up the river and raked the wood from end to end with salvoes from our guns. I have always wanted to see the bulbfields of Holland, and here they were at their best. Lovely lakes of colour filled the landscape and it really was a most inspiring sight.

Dotted round the fields there were lots of dark blobs, and if you looked thru' field glasses, you could see what they were — wrecked German aeroplanes. Nature and civilisation mixed together, and they didn't mix very well.

It is difficult to believe how desperate the Germans seem to have been, and how many aeroplanes they lost, but I saw with my own eyes, in just about six square

14

miles of country, at least thirty wrecks, only one of which was Belgian. The others were Junkers 52 troop carriers, and they had just been landed as best as they could. Some were only slightly damaged, the others burnt up or smashed to bits.

When we had finished our bombarding, we went back, and on the way a flight of six Heinkel 111's came over the wood and left what looked like a cloud of soap bubbles, but which were parachute troops. The Germans were using Messerschmitt 110, Heinkel 111, and Junkers 88, so it was rather interesting. That night we posted guards on the jetty, as it was thought the Germans might try and rush us. At dawn the next morning we left to meet some more destroyers who were bringing a lot of Marines over, and after that we went on Patrol.

Just as we were in the narrow part of the channel where there was no room to manoeuvre, there was a roar, and out of the sun shot a hun, before we had time to realise what had happened, there was a whistle as the bombs came towards us, and then all round us enormous explosions. One only missed by about 5 yards, but very little damage was done luckily.

A few hours later we sighted a Dutch liner, and when we were about a mile away from her, out of the clouds shot 3 dive bombers, and despite the barrage we put up, she was left blazing and listing heavily.

We rushed up to her and found she was a trooper carrying Dutch and English troops, who were now jumping overboard.

We picked up practically all of them, some being drowned, and took them back to the Hook.

That night we joined the flotilla which took Juliana and Co over, but left it later to go back to Dover. In fact a very hectic weekend. One begins to appreciate what Finland and Norway have been going thru' when the air raid warning is sounding practically all the time, as it was at the Hague and the Hook. When we left however, the air seemed to have become British, and there were large patrols of British machines flying round.

Well I don't suppose we shall go back there again, as

15

the new boats have got there by now.

The Jerries dropped lots of magnetic mines round our river, and in the channel our sweepers exploded five. It is lucky we are de-magnetised. Well I must stop now.

Your loving son
Michael

If the Captain had known that he had a budding war correspondent in Mess 5, smuggling uncensored letters ashore, he might well have changed his mind about recommending me for officer training!

HMS Wild Swan's last action, from the Daily Telegraph:

The 1,120 ton British destroyer *Wild Swan*, as reported in this paper last Saturday, destroyed six of 12 JU.88 bombers which attacked the ship 100 miles west of the French coast.

The ship, damaged by bombs, could not avoid a collision with a Spanish trawler disabled by the raiders. The fishing vessel sank and three other Spanish trawlers were victims of the Nazis. The *Wild Swan* later sank. Her crew were picked up by another destroyer.

CHAPTER 2

Midshipman

Whilst at Chatham I received my papers to go to the Officers' Training Base, HMS *King Alfred*, at Hove in Sussex.

This was certainly a big change from being an ordinary seaman on the lower deck of a destroyer and for the first time I found that I was with a lot of other young men who had been selected to train as officers on a three months' course which was both interesting and enjoyable.

We lived in an underground car park in large dormitories with two-tier beds, but it was nice to be on shore again. It was certainly more spacious than the lower deck, and we could go ashore in Brighton with its many attractions.

By this time France had fallen, the British Army had been taken off from Dunkirk, everything looked very black, and it was felt that Britain would be invaded in due course by the German Army.

Therefore one of our duties was to be taken up to the South Downs at night together with a rifle and several rounds of ammunition, to be Britain's first line of defence!

However, being young and enthusiastic the appalling war situation that we were in went right over my head and I eventually passed out as a midshipman, with my pay increased to 5 shillings per day, and my first posting to the armed merchant cruiser *Cilicia*, which was stationed up in Greenock in Scotland.

Cilicia was a fine modern liner, which, with her sister ship, *Circassia*, had been built for the liner trade between the UK and Bombay. As an armed merchant cruiser she had been fitted with eight 6″ guns, four on either side of the ship, and also some light anti-aircraft guns. There was no fire control system so that each gun had to be aimed and fired separately and there was no radar or ASDIC. The theory of the armed merchant cruiser was that it gave a convoy some protection against surface ships such as German raiders but she would have been a sitting target for submarines or aircraft, or against a "pocket Battle Ship" such as the Germans were deploying in the Atlantic. It would be just a matter of time before she was sunk, and this is what happened to the Jervis Bay, which went down in heroic circumstances and earned its captain the V.C.

On joining the ship I found myself in the Gunroom Mess, along with a number of young men of a similar age, and I shared a luxurious cabin with another RNVR midshipman called Peter Liddell. One of my duties while the ship was at Greenock was to drive the Captain's "skimmer". This was a fast planing motorboat and of course was quite up my street. Unfortunately one day I ran it ashore and knocked the propeller off when the engine stuck in gear, and as a punishment I was sent up the main mast of the ship, to sit on the yardarm for a number of hours.

Whilst on board the *Cilicia* we did two convoys from the Clyde to Gibraltar and back, and whilst at sea we kept watches and had navigational lessons and practical navigation using a sextant, for sun and star sights.

It was nice to leave blacked out and cold Scotland with all the wartime shortages and finding ourselves arriving in warm weather at Gibraltar with all its lights on at night. It was exciting going ashore because the place had an African/Mediterranean flavour, there were shops full of goods, and it was just like being back in pre-war times.

The only excitement that we had on the convoy trips was when we were attacked by a long range German Condor aircraft. It tried to bomb us but luckily the bombs missed, but it strafed the ship with cannon fire causing casualties to one of the gun's crew with one killed.

I experienced my first burial at sea with the body stitched up in a weighted canvas bag, and at the committal stage, the body was tipped over the side. I was told that it was naval custom when sewing a body up in a canvas bag to always put the last stitch through the nose. The theory was that if the person was still alive he would sit up and say "ough".

We must have been approaching the end of 1940 when the second of these convoys brought us back to Greenock, and after some leave I found that I had an appointment to go as First Lieutenant to a coastal forces vessel, ML 145, which was building down at Looe in Cornwall.

CHAPTER 3

Coastal Forces

I spent a pleasant six weeks or so living in lodgings in the lovely Cornish port of Looe while the vessel was completed at the yard of Curtiss, a well known yacht builder.

The Commanding Officer of the vessel was a Lieut. Hellings, RNVR, a solicitor who had been a keen yachtsman, and I found him a nice person to work for.

The MLs were designed to be all purpose patrol vessels. They were 112′ long by 18′ beam and they could be built by yacht builders round the coast, as they were built of double skinned mahogany. They were round bilged and therefore rolled alarmingly at sea, and they had two petrol engines which gave them a speed of 18 knots. They had a simple form of ASDIC which only operated either dead ahead or on either beam so that instead of moving the ASDIC beam to search, the boat itself had to alter course and sweep the sea ahead. The armament consisted of an old 6 pounder gun from the First World War, some Lewis machine guns, about 12 depth charges and an extraordinary apparatus called a Holman projector which was supposed to be the anti-aircraft protection.

This Heath Robinson affair had a barrel which was connected to a high pressure air cylinder and it was loaded with a topless tin can in which there was a hand grenade. When it was fired the compressed air blew the tin out up to about 200–300 feet, when the tin can fell off and the grenade exploded. It could only be effective against a very low flying aircraft and it would need a great deal of luck for the grenade to go off anywhere near the aircraft.

It was a most ridiculous piece of equipment, but we had fun sometimes, firing potatoes at each other's boats. Several hundred MLs were built during the war and, although it was designed for anti-submarine work, that was probably its most unsuitable use, but as a general patrol boat it saw a lot of service and did a lot of good.

We finally commissioned ML 145 and went from Looe round to Dartmouth, where we were to be based to begin with. Dartmouth is a beautiful place and I much enjoyed being there and we used to go out for exercises off the coast, and life could not really have been pleasanter, in the circumstances.

However, the pleasantness ended when the Germans bombed Plymouth. From where we were in Dartmouth we could see the whole sky lit up by the flames, and hear the bombs and the guns, as Plymouth was more or less destroyed.

We were eventually ordered round to the east coast to be based at Harwich to do coastal convoy work.

The First Lieutenant of one of the other MLs in our Flotilla was David Budworth, an interesting young man who had been to Dartmouth as a cadet but left the Navy and had now come back as an RNVR midshipman. I knew him for many years after the war when he set himself up as an engineer and designed jet engines, and also built yachts, and he was eventually killed flying. I remember that he had a motorbike on board his ML which he used to take to bits and stow in the engine room, and this, when we were in harbour, gave us some mobility.

ML 145 and 150 eventually immortalised themselves, their officers and crews, when they engaged an E-boat in the North Sea in September 1943, and sank it by ramming it!

After some months I was posted from 145 to a Coastal Force course in motor gunboats which was held up in Scotland at Fort William. This again was a nice change as the MGBs were much more interesting and attractive

Bow of ML150 after ramming and sinking an E-boat

MGB 90 at speed

Captain's view from the Bridge of MGB 90

than the slow MLs.

At that time, Motor Gunboats were intended to escort Motor Torpedo boats in their offensive role against enemy shipping, to protect them from escort vessels, rather as fighter aircraft escorted bombers.

As the German E-boats began to attack our coastal convoys, the MGBs developed a new defensive-offensive role against the E-boat, firstly trying to intercept them as they approached our coasts, and then lying in wait for them, off their home ports, as they returned, often damaged, tired and off guard. These tactics proved very successful.

As our MTB attacks on enemy shipping were stepped up, the Germans increased the size and number of their convoy escorts, and it was realised that the MGBs didn't have enough fire power to sink the bigger escorts, which they could do, if they had their own torpedoes.

So the concept of the MGB with torpedoes was born, and from 1943, the 71' 6" MGB hulls were strengthened, and fitted with two torpedoes, and changed their names.

Two MTBs crossing the moon path.
Oilpainting by Lieut. R. M. Barge, DSC, RNVR

My last boat, MGB 121, became MTB 440.

This proved a very successful development and the MGB/MTBs sank many enemy ships with their new armament.

After the course I was appointed as First Lieutenant to MGB 90 which was commanded by a Canadian called Corny Burke. MGB 90 was one of a Flotilla of American MTBs which had had their torpedoes removed and had been given to the Navy as part of Lease-Lend and shipped over to Liverpool.

They were lovely looking boats and very fast, doing about 45 knots, and very well equipped with everything except effective guns.

I went with Corny Burke up to Liverpool to collect our boat together with another crew who were collecting a similar boat, and then we had an enjoyable passage down

MGB 90, on passage from Liverpool to Portland
Corny Burke and the Coxswain

The MGB Flotilla in Hamilton Dock, Lowestoft

We practised close station keeping, at speed

American power-operated turrets

the west coast, round Lands End and up to Portland Harbour. We had calm weather all the way and it was a wonderful feeling to be travelling at about 40 knots in this beautiful boat during the day and spending the night in some small fishing port, rather like a yachting cruise.

Driving a MGB or MTB is an exhilarating experience. As the three throttles are opened there is a tremendous roar from the straight through exhausts, like an aircraft taking off, and also like an aircraft, the boat levels off as she gains speed, until she is skimming the surface of the water, instead of going through it, and there is a great sense of speed.

This is quite comfortable on a smooth sea, but if there are waves, and if the boat is going into the sea, then she crashes and bangs on the waves, and it is necessary to stand with bent knees to absorb the shocks.

Going down wind in a sea is even more exciting, especially if the waves have built up. The boat surfs down the front of the wave at an increased speed, and then buries its bows in the next wave, throwing out a great fan of white water on either side, and then labours like an old bus as she climbs up the other side and shoots off the top and down the next wave face, and so on.

You have to hold on all the time, and the Coxwain has a hard job to keep her running straight, and prevent her broaching to in the troughs.

A trick that the Coxswains soon learned was that, when keeping close station on the quarter of another boat, the speed of the boat could be varied, without touching the throttles, by moving into or away from the front of the leading boat's wake. This was like going down the face of a wave, and she would increase her speed until you took her away from the wake again.

At Portland the remainder of the Flotilla were already there, under the command of Lieut. Bremer Horne, RN, and we proceeded to do exercises and also to have the boats fitted with additional guns. Corny Burke was a great person to be First Lieutenant to, and he was probably the first Canadian that I had ever met. He was young and enthusiastic and came from Vancouver, and was supposed to have left his young wife behind, but he had managed to smuggle her over and she was good fun too.

One of the other Commanding Officers in the Flotilla was Ronald Chesney. He was bearded, large and fat and looked like Henry VIII and his eating habits were also very similar. He was reputed to have been tried in Scotland before the war for murdering his mother but found not guilty. He was certainly a very rough man, and he hit the headlines at the end of the war when he was involved in smuggling in Europe and eventually committed suicide when the police were about to catch him. A rum fellow for a colleague!

One day in Portland our boat was lying alongside Chesney's boat, and one of the ratings on the other boat was cleaning a gun and accidentally fired it, and the bullet went into a box of 20 mm Oerlikon ammunition which was sitting on the deck of our boat above the petrol tanks. The ammunition box exploded, blowing in the decks and the petrol tanks, and both boats went up spectacularly in flames.

Luckily nobody was injured by the explosion but in view of the fierceness of the fire we had to leave rather quickly over the side and swim to the dock, losing all our possessions.

It was at Weymouth or Portland that I first met Rodney Sykes who was in an MTB Flotilla. Together, we bought our first car, which cost us £15.

It gave us essential mobility in the evenings, but there was one major snag — we had no petrol to run it on.

We thought about the thousands of gallons our boats devoured on operations, and we decided that "His Majesty" wouldn't really miss a few gallons for our car, which, if we had been caught, would have been a most heinous crime.

Hamilton Dock, Lowestoft, with the 7th Flotilla Boats in the middle ground

Ronnie Barge

So at the dead of one dark night, we drove the car down to the dock, and while Rodney extracted some petrol from one of our boats, I kept guard at the inner end of the dock, and the arrangement was that if I sighted anyone I should whistle the tune of "There were 27 babies at the Baby Show".

Luckily this was never necessary, and our car took us all over the place.

Corny Burke and I became a "spare crew" after the loss of 90 and with the balance of the six boats in the Flotilla were sent up to Lowestoft on the east coast. Our base there was in Hamilton Dock along with some MLs and other naval vessels, and we lived ashore in the Royal Hotel which was the Officers Mess, on the other side of the town.

Our boats were fitted with a quick firing 2 pounder aft, and we were mostly engaged in anti E-boat patrols, the E-boats coming across from Holland to attack our east coast convoys.

We had occasional German air raids on Lowestoft and we used to be able to put up quite a good barrage from Hamilton Dock, but I don't think we ever hit anything nor was there damage caused to our boats. Occasionally, for practice, a Naval aircraft would tow a drogue, out to seaward, for us to shoot at. It was reputed that one pilot radioed back after a near miss — "please note that I am pulling the drogue, not pushing it".

We had some nice people in our Flotilla and morale was excellent, and whilst we spent many weary hours at sea, we had very few engagements with the Germans at that time, although we occasionally went across to the Dutch coast, helping escort the MTBs from Felixstowe, when they were attacking German convoys.

Felixstowe also had a Flotilla of MGBs commanded by the famous Lieut. Commander Robert Hichens, DSO, DSC. He developed new ideas for the joint use of gun boats and torpedo boats and became very successful in Coastal Forces. When I was down in Felixstowe I became friends with his First Lieutenant, a nice young man called Francis Head.

Sadly Hichens was later killed in action and Francis had an accident with his motorbike and was killed.

In our Flotilla I particularly remember Derek Leaf and Tom Sadleir, who became good friends but sadly were both later killed in action.

From Lowestoft I was appointed as First Lieutenant to Ronnie Barge, who had just been given command of MGB 9 in the Flotilla commanded by Lieut. Dick Richards, RN, based at Ramsgate, but operating from Dover.

MGB 9 was a 70' Power boat and Ronnie was slightly older than myself, charming, artistic and a most attractive personality.

At Ramsgate we lived in the Yacht Club which was on the harbour and the boats were moored alongside the wall in the lower harbour, which was tidal. Although we were based in Ramsgate, our operational base was Dover, and we would run down there in the evenings before going to sea on operations.

Our operations from Dover were mainly in support of the MTB Flotilla based there, which was very active, as enemy shipping was constantly moving between Boulogne, Calais and beyond, and was monitored by the early radar installations on the cliffs at Dover.

We would be called out to support the MTBs in attacks on this shipping.

There was also the odd "clandestine" job to do, to land agents on the enemy coast on dark nights.

We would be sent to pick up an anonymous looking man in a mackintosh and trilby hat, off the end of a jetty. He would sit on the mess deck, without speaking, until we had crossed the Channel and crept in to some remote part of the Belgian coast, when he would be rowed ashore in a dinghy, and disappeared into the darkness with his attache case.

We felt very nervous while we waited for the dinghy to come back, we could have been attacked from seaward by a patrolling vessel, or from the shore, and it was a relief when we were able to head out to sea again, on our silenced engines.

I used to feel very sorry for these agents, and wonder what happened to them — perhaps a shot in the darkness, and it was all over. If so, next time the Germans would be waiting for us.

By this time I had had my 20th birthday and therefore was promoted from Midshipman to Sub-Lieutenant, and whilst I was still 20 I was given my first command to MGB 42 also operating from Ramsgate.

MGB 42 was a 63' Power boat with two Rolls Royce Merlin engines, a Marine version of the same engine that powered the Spitfires and Hurricanes, so slightly smaller than MGB 9, and only had one power operated twin ·5 machine gut turret amidships, as against the two, one on either side of the bridge, which the bigger boats had. She also had Lewis guns and a single Oerlikon 20 mm gun aft.

My First Lieutenant was a young Welshman by the name of Graham Hughes, and a very nice person he was. I was very proud to have command of my own boat and on the basis that pride cometh before a fall, I fell fairly quickly.

In MGBs we had developed a technique to attack enemy shipping by crossing the target ship's bow at speed and dropping a depth charge at the vital moment so that it exploded under the ship, and obviously timing was the essence of the whole operation, and it was necessary to practise this. We used therefore to practise when we could on friendly ships, and one day when I was doing this on a trawler up on the east coast, I didn't realise how narrow the channel was, and we hit a mudbank on the other side of the target ship and damaged our propellers.

So with my tail between my legs we had to go up to Brightlingsea, for the boat to be repaired.

Ramsgate, with MGBs alongside the harbour arm. In the foreground — 63′ MGBs of the Free Polish Navy who worked with us

Elco boats, 7th MGB Flotilla based at Lowestoft

34

Brightlingsea was not much of a place and we felt rather frustrated kicking our heels up there and doing nothing. Whilst there I celebrated my 21st birthday and I can remember that my father sent me a bottle of champagne and that Graham and I drank this in the cockpit of the boat that evening.

Eventually the repairs were completed but we then found ourselves still hanging around while officialdom considered where we were to go.

Being young and impetuous I decided that we would make the decision ourselves, and as Felixstowe, the famous MTB and MGB base commanded by Lieut. Commander Hichens, was at the mouth of Harwich Harbour, I decided that we would go there, to report. So we proceeded to slip our moorings and go down there, without getting the prior permission of the local Naval Officer in Charge.

This of course upset officialdom considerably and signals started flying in all directions, and I was asked why we had left without permission, etc., etc. In fact officialdom was so upset that I was ordered to report to the Rear Admiral Coastal Forces in London to explain myself.

With considerable trepidation I went to the office of Rear Admiral Piers Kekewich, RN, who looked sternly at me and said "Why did you sail from Brightlingsea without orders?"

As a young officer in the 1914-18 War, Rear Admiral Kekewich had himself been in command of an MTB in Russia. He therefore understood when I said "Sir, I wanted to get my boat back to the Flotilla as quickly as possible so that we could resume active service."

Very precocious on my part, but it worked and eventually after a fatherly chat from him I was sent back to Felixstowe and nothing more was said about my misconduct.

Eventually we got back to Ramsgate and resumed service with the Flotilla.

There were two other 63 foot MGBs in Ramsgate, both of them manned by Poles from the Free Polish Navy. Poor things, they had nothing left from the overrun of their country, and their hate of the Germans was very intense. They used to sit on deck sharpening their cutlasses, and they never brought prisoners back after an action.

We also had a French boat and in our Flotilla, a Frenchman called Roger King (we called him "Le Roi"), and two Dutch MTBs in Dover, so we were quite a cosmopolitan and international group.

Unfortunately we had a further accident in MGB 42, in Dover Harbour one day when, with another boat, we were proceeding at speed across the harbour and we found ourselves planing inadvertently on the wake of the other boat, in which position the boat became temporarily unsteerable, and we hit a large destroyer mooring buoy. This put a big hole in the bow, and as repairs would take some time, she was de-commissioned.

I have recently discovered that my first Commanding Officer in MGBs, Corny Burke, had previously been the navigator of MGB 42 in March 1941, when she was badly damaged by a mine, whilst coming into Penzance.

Corny wrote: "The blowing up of MGB 42 off Penzance was clearly my fault. The CO asked me for a course into Penzance. The course I gave went smack over a mine, the location of which had been promulgated. The Senior Naval Officer, Penzance, a World War One Commander RN, came down to the beached wreck of the boat and said, 'Subby, I witnessed the explosion of that acoustic mine, and I know you were right where you shouldn't have been. However, for your sake, I will report that you were not where I know you were!' "

What a wise decision that turned out to be, not to "tarnish" Corny's record. Corny went on to be a most successful Commanding Officer of "D" class MGBs in the Mediterranean, where he led a unit of boats, on the west coast of Italy, and in the Adriatic, whose Commanding

Free Polish MGBs at Ramsgate

70′ Power Boat MGB — replaced by the 71′ 6″ MGB
The cliffs of Dover in the background

Officers were all Canadians from Vancouver, and which wreaked havoc among the German supply ships to their garrisons in the islands, and earned Corny three DSCs. Their exploits are vividly described by Corny's First Lieutenant, Leonard Reynolds DSC, in his book "MGB 658".

The experiences of MGB 42 suggest that I was quite unfit to have a command at the tender age of 21 and perhaps this was true, but there was also an element of bad luck.

In the same context I can remember being with Dick Richards on his boat (MGB 107) one day in the Channel off Dover, when we saw another naval vessel coming in the opposite direction, and Dick said, "Let's practise a depth charge attack on him". So we closed him at speed, on opposite courses, intending to cross his bow very close and drop an imaginary depth charge under him, but at the last minute the captain of the other vessel panicked and started to alter course away, which resulted in us having an almighty collision and both boats being very seriously damaged.

Dick was quite self-possessed about it and said, "We've made a mistake, we have to practise these manoeuvres, and there's always a risk of something going wrong, but there is no point in there being a witch hunt, therefore we will report it as an accident due to failure of our steering."

He then called the motor mechanic up and told him to remove the connecting pin on the steering and drop it in the bilge underneath, and when we got back to harbour and this was found, it was accepted that this was the cause of the unfortunate accident. While MGB 107 was being repaired, Dick commissioned a new boat, MGB 110.

These very beamy boats, with a light displacement, were also very difficult to steer at slow speed, therefore we used to manoeuvre at about 10 knots, which then caused quite a lot of wash from the boat.

On another occasion, when entering Portsmouth

7th Flotilla boats in Line ahead

Harbour and passing HMS *Dolphin*, the submarine base, I was later sent for by Rear Admiral (Submarines) and given a dressing down, because he said I had entered harbour too fast, and my wash "had knocked a Wren off the casing of a submarine"! I never saw the poor girl.

After MGB 42 was paid off, I was given command of MGB 10, and my new First Lieutenant was Colin Thomas, Graham Hughes having become a spare CO to the Flotilla.

Colin came from Cheshire and had qualified as an accountant. After the war he continued in accountancy and eventually became the Secretary of Lloyd's of London, so that I kept up with him for many years.

I remember one incident when we were on operations and we were carrying Roger King as the senior officer for that night, and Colin was doing the navigation, and at one point had to admit that he wasn't quite sure where we were off the enemy coast. When he told this to Roger King, Roger's angry comment to me was "Then why is he a Sub-Lieutenant?" Whenever I met Colin again after the war, we used to repeat this comment in a French accent. I don't think that Roger King was his proper French name, but we called him this because, at the time, his girlfriend was a Mrs King.

We had a certain amount of mechanical trouble with the old 70′ Power boats and sometimes we were out of action for a day or two, when, if there was an operation, we would go to sea in other people's boats as supernumeraries to help. On several of these occasions I went with Dick Richards, and usually it would be an exciting night because one never quite knew what he was going to do. On one of these occasions I remember that we crept almost into Boulogne Harbour without being detected, looking for a target.

I have always been rather keen on flying and used to go up to the aerodrome at Manston where there was a Fleet Air Arm Squadron of torpedo-carrying Albacores. These antique biplanes were developed from the Swordfish, and could do at least 90 knots! The Squadron Leader's navigator was a keen squash player and I used to go up there to play squash with him, and if a plane was going up for a test flight or some other reason, I used to go for a ride in the air gunner's seat.

One evening when I was up there, the Squadron was alerted and told to take off immediately to attack an enemy ship which had been detected by Dover Radar coming up the French coast near Boulogne.

Impetuous as usual, I asked the Squadron Leader whether I could come with him and he said "Yes, but we are leaving immediately and you must borrow a parachute, but if you are not ready in time, we shall leave and you can go in one of the other aircraft." Getting my parachute took a little time and therefore I missed the Squadron Leader's plane and found myself in another plane with an unknown pilot and crew. We took off for the French coast and eventually flew low over Boulogne and were heavily fired at, but never found the enemy ship and finally returned to Manston.

There we heard the awful news that the Squadron Leader's plane was missing, assumed shot down in the Channel, and I immediately returned to Dover, to my boat, because we were then ordered out to search for any survivors.

Nothing was ever found, so I had had a lucky escape, but as usual I got into trouble with my senior officers for having gone out on an operational flight, which was against all orders. It would seem that discipline was not my strongest feature, but that I enjoyed good luck.

The officers and crew of ML 150 looking pleased with themselves
after sinking an E-boat by ramming.
Hamilton Dock, Lowestoft.

CHAPTER 4

Bill Fesq

I shall always remember Bill Fesq, the tall, quiet Australian who became my First Lieutenant in December 1942. I had been appointed to command MGB 113, a brand new 71' 6" Power boat, built at the company's factory at Hythe, near Southampton.

Our Flotilla was being re-equipped with this new, faster and more powerfully armed boat, and Dick Richards had taken delivery of the first new boat, MGB 107.

Our new boat must have been the fourth in the Flotilla, and we would have gone down to Southampton, with our crew, and carried out acceptance trials, before signing for her, and setting out westwards to Weymouth, where the training base was located.

There, we would have spent 5 − 6 weeks, getting to know each other, and the new boat, gunnery practice at moving targets, navigational exercises by day and night, and practising high speed, close station keeping, and attack formations.

The new boats had three supercharged Packard petrol engines of 1,350 h.p. each, a maximum speed of about 43 knots in smooth water, but they could also run silently, with underwater exhausts, at about 10 knots, which was valuable in surprise night attacks.

On the foredeck was a 2 pounder "Pom Pom" in a power operated turret, which fired shells at about 120 rounds per minute, and amidships behind the bridge was another power operated turret, with twin 20 mm Oerlikon guns, with a high rate of fire.

Bill Fesq

Either side of the bridge was a pair of machine guns, and on deck were two depth charges.

The wheelhouse forward of the bridge was the navigator's position (the First Lieutenant) and the boat was steered from the bridge by the Coxswain, under the control of the Commanding Officer who also worked the three throttles and engine controls. The close concentration and co-operation of the Commanding Officer and Coxswain were needed to keep the boat in station, on either quarter of the lead boat, at speed and only feet distant, by day or night.

There were normally two officers, plus a third under training on operations, and about fourteen crew comprising gunners and their mates, engine room staff, and a radio operator.

On completion of our working up period, we proceeded up channel to Ramsgate, to rejoin the Flotilla. There were normally eight boats in a Flotilla and there were two Flotillas at Ramsgate, so it was a busy little port. The boats lay, about three boats alongside each other, under the protection of the high stone harbour wall.

The crews lived on board, and the officers lived in the yacht club on the north side of the harbour.

We were under the operational control of Vice Admiral Dover, about 25 miles away. We would either set out on operations from Ramsgate, or go down first to Dover, where the MTBs were based, to go on a joint operation, or spend the night there at 15 minutes' notice to go to sea, if required. On the latter basis, the First Lieutenant and crew slept on the boats, and the Commanding Officers in a dormitory at the base, above the Ferry dock where the boats lay.

If we were called out — we slept fully dressed — we would go sleepily into the operations room, to receive our orders, while the crews got the main engines running, and we would then jump down on board — ". . . let go forward, let go aft . . .' — and off we would go in a matter of minutes, trying to see in the darkness. These operations would always be at night as we were vulnerable to aircraft during the day.

It was an exhausting and an exciting life (although there could be long periods of boredom, when the weather was bad) but we were all young — I was 22 in April 1943 — and there was a great *esprit de corps* amongst us.

We had the greatest loyalty and respect for our senior officer, Dick Richards, and would have gone anywhere with him. He was a regular Navy Lieutenant of about 24, married with a young son, and totally dedicated to his job of making his Flotilla a scourge to the Germans on the other side of the Channel.

Bill's duties, as First Lieutenant, were to keep the charts and code books updated, deal with any crew problems, see that the guns and engines were properly maintained, top up fuel and ammunition, and any other job necessary to keep the boat ready for sea and operations. When we were in action his duties were also to control the guns. We would go to sea to practise gunnery and other routines, at regular intervals. If we knew that we were going to sea that evening, we would work only in the forenoons and relax in the afternoons. Among the other Commanding Officers in the Flotilla were Ronnie Barge, Philip Lee and Arthur Outen, all of whom made their mark in the Battle of the Narrow Seas, and we were a "band of brothers" in true Naval tradition, together with the other officers and crew members.

In a defensive role, our enemies were the German E-boats, which attacked our convoys with torpedoes, and R-boats, which laid mines in our shipping lanes.

Our major role though, at Dover, was an offensive one, to escort our MTBs in attacks on enemy merchant shipping on the French, Belgian and Dutch coasts, together with their well armed escorts, who fought to protect them.

At a later date our targets also became armed trawlers and "flak ships", which were stationed on the enemy shipping lanes to intercept our MTBs and MGBs at night, and our low flying aircraft by day.

The E-boats were formidable foes, they were long and low, better sea boats than ours in bad weather, and diesel powered, so they didn't have the same fire risk as our petrol engined boats. They fought hard like the German U-boats, and they were probably better all round fighting machines than our boats.

The R-boats were more like our MLs and were mostly used for escort and minelaying work — they didn't have the speed of the E-boats, but they were heavily armed.

We usually operated in units of three or four boats, either going to sea in the evenings to sit on the enemy's shipping lanes with a hydrophone to listen for approaching shipping or marauding E-boats (sometimes we would be startled when shells from the shore batteries would suddenly send up water spouts around us) or to try and intercept E-boats coming across to, or coming home from, our shipping lanes. At other times, when Dover

Radar detected an enemy convoy coming up their coast, all available MTBs and MGBs would be sent out to mount an attack. I remember one apparently valuable enemy ship had an escort of no fewer than 24 ships to protect her.

It was coming back from one of these patrols, as the sun began to rise, and one's thoughts turned to breakfast, that a sixth sense made me look astern, and flying up our wake was a German fighter. I dropped to the bottom of the cockpit instinctively, as machine gun bullets hit the front of the cockpit where I had been standing . Nobody saw it, and nobody fired back, it all happened so quickly, but it was a lesson to be learned — always be alert!

Throughout the beginning of the war, I always had a particular personal worry — "How would I behave in action? Would I be paralysed with fright and show myself, in front of others, to be a coward?"

I felt that as I had had a better start in life, and a better education than many others, it was my duty to set an example, but could I do it, when it came to the real test?

The real test came one summer evening, when I was a spare CO and riding in Dick Richards' boat, going down from Ramsgate to Dover. We were suddenly alerted that a force of E-boats and R-boats had been spotted coming across to our convoy route off Dover, and in a matter of minutes we saw them and closed them at speed.

They were obviously going to lay mines, and were in line ahead. Dick brought his boats up their starboard side at close range, and we opened fire. We concentrated our fire on the last boats in the line, one of which was badly hit and slowed down. It was still just daylight and we closed to about 100 yards, exchanging a fierce barrage of fire, and I found myself on the after deck, with a Lewis gun, firing from the hip, and seeing my tracer bullets streaming into the R-boat's hull, along with the pounding from our main armament, and I realised then that I wasn't paralysed with fright, in fact I was shouting and experiencing a savage elation and sense of relief. The action ended with the surrender of the R-boat and its surviving crew. I had passed my test.

Dick, who always wanted to bring a "Prize" back to Dover, picked up the swimmers, put his First Lieutenant and some of the crew on board, who attached a tow rope and returned on board. The R-boat was by now burning, and presumably visible to the German shore batteries, because shells began to drop around us.

Then, as more shells exploded in the water nearby, the prisoners began to get very excited and pointed to the mines still on the deck of the R-boat, which, if hit, might have gone up in a spectacular explosion.

Dick quickly realised that it was a very dangerous situation, and sent me aft, with an axe, to cut the tow rope. I missed several times before achieving this, which didn't improve the after deck, but we got away safely and back to Dover, and delivered our prisoners to the Army.

It was on another patrol one night, off Cap Gris Nez, looking for enemy shipping, that we had a very narrow escape. We were with Dick Richards leading, and Ronnie Barge in line astern and at half speed, when we felt a terrible bump on our bow which made the whole boat shudder. I throttled down and immediately thought of mines (we had recently lost a boat, blown in half by a mine) but it must have been a large piece of wreckage.

When the boat had stopped, Bill went forward and reported that we were badly holed in the forepeak, and making water. The other two boats had by then disappeared into the darkness, unaware of what had happened to us until we were able to radio them, and then they couldn't find us.

It was only slowly that we realised the full horror of our plight. We were on our own, only miles from the French coast. We were so far down by the bow that our stern was partly out of the water, which meant that the cooling water inlets for the engines were also out of the water, and that we couldn't run the engines, so we couldn't get under

Prisoners from sunken E-boats

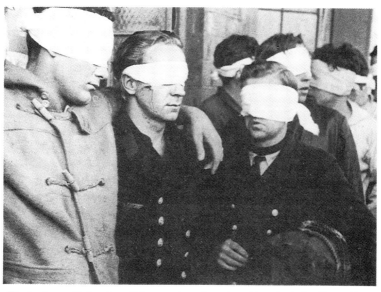

Their faces diplay bewilderment and resignation, but for them the
war is over. What happened to them in the peace?

way and head for home, and with the main engines out of action, we had no hydraulic power for the gun turrets, so we couldn't defend ourselves, other than with the bridge machine guns.

We managed to get a wireless signal through to Dover, and then all we could do was to wait and see what would happen — perhaps the Germans would send a patrol boat out to get us. It began to get light, and soon we could see the headland of Cap Gris Nez quite clearly. Some of the crew said — looking at the coast — "at least we aren't too far from home". Bill and I decided not to tell them it wasn't home!

The sea was calm, and we lay quietly in a slight swell. Suddenly there was a "whooshing" noise, an explosion, and a great spout of water.

We all knew what that was, and there was nothing we could do about it either. Shelling from the shore batteries continued for some time. I don't remember for how long, but whilst some shells landed quite close, we were not hit or damaged.

And then we were suddenly cheered up, as two fighters appeared overhead and circled us, their pilots waving. They were RAF Typhoons and we were no longer alone, our morale went up. They would report our position and protect us. But the interlude was all too short. The shelling had stopped, and then out of the blue came the Messerschmitts. We had hardly realised what was happening when we suddenly saw both our Typhoon escorts dive into the sea, as they were jumped by the Germans, out of the sun.

Both pilots must have been killed instantly, and we felt awful that they had died violent deaths for us. And then it was our turn — flying low over the sea, their eight guns firing, the sea around us erupted into spray, and there was nothing we could do other than fire off our inadequate machine guns. After several runs at us, they disappeared and it was eerily quiet again.

Bill, as one would expect, was cool and collected. We surveyed the boat for damage, which was only slight, and luckily we were all uninjured, but shaken. What was going to happen next?

I don't remember how long afterwards it was, but we gradually became aware of more planes above us, and then we realised that they were ours. The RAF, angered by the loss of its Typhoons, was putting an "umbrella" above us, and then it was that we spotted on the horizon, coming towards us from England, two of our boats at speed.

It was Dick Richards and Ronnie Barge coming back to find us, and what a welcome sight they were.

They soon closed us, a tow rope was secured, and we began the long slow haul back to home and safety, while the RAF seemed to fill the sky above us.

Once through the gap in the minefield, a tug was waiting to take over the tow, and we made faster progress back to Dover, and as we came through the harbour entrance, a message from the Admiral was flashed to us — "Welcome home".

Our damaged bow was soon repaired and we rejoined the Flotilla at Ramsgate.

It was a busy spring and summer that year.

The Germans stepped up their attacks on our shipping, and the mining of our shipping lanes, and they strengthened the defence of their own shipping lanes, with more escort vessels and more flak trawlers on patrol.

This meant more operations for us and the Dover MTBs, and contact with the enemy forces was frequent. We also did some minelaying sorties on their coasts, and cleared some of the moored mines they had laid on our side.

We found that if we went out in daylight at low water spring tides, we could actually see some of their mines on the surface.

With a rifle or a machine gun, one got a most satisfactory confirmation of a bullseye, as a great spout of

51

water rose into the air!

We knew a little about mines because the previous year the Flotilla had been supplied with a quantity of small mines, joined together by ropes which floated. The mines, which also floated, contained about 50 pounds of explosive and were detonated by evil looking horns on the top, and our boats were fitted with a twin railed track on each quarter, holding 9 mines each and leading over the transom.

The idea was to drop these mines in a long line, across the path of an enemy convoy, when, if a ship steamed into the floating ropes, they drew the mines alongside and exploded them on the water-line, and hopefully sank it.

This machiavellian weapon was apparently "over" from the 1914-18 war, and was said to be a brainchild of Churchill's.

Laying them in action was quite another matter. Having loaded each boat with 18 mines, and carefully secured the 100 ft of rope between each mine, so that it hopefully didn't snag on anything, we proceeded to sea to get in position on the edge of the enemy convoy lane off the French coast, and then to stop and listen on our hydrophones for the sound of enemy shipping.

Having established that ships were coming towards us, we proceeded at slow speed on silenced engines across the convoy lane, the leader deciding when each boat should lay its mines. This was a hair-raising experience for the First Lieutenant, and when our turn came, my job was to push the first mine off the transom, hoping its rope wouldn't get entangled with anything, and keeping clear of its horns. As the rope ran out and tightened, it would suddenly pull the next mine rattling down the rails in a shower of sparks and into the sea, until, with great relief, they were all gone. We never knew whether they ever sank anything, but luckily we had no accidents, and I was glad when the supply of them ran out.

Because of our night attacks on their shipping and

escorts, the Germans became very jumpy, and began shooting in every direction when we attacked them. Once this started, they seemed quite unable to distinguish between friend and foe, and many a time, after we had attacked, successfully or otherwise, we would retire to seaward and stop, and watch with amazement, as the German ships continued to shoot at each other for minutes on end — it was the best fireworks display any of us had ever seen, and they must have inflicted a lot of damage and casualties on themselves.

One evening in March 1943, when we were on short notice at Dover, we were "scrambled" to accompany the MTBs in an attack on a small convoy, that Dover Radar had detected, stealing eastwards up the French coast. There were only two gunboats (Dick in 110 and ourselves in 113) and three MTBs.

On reaching the enemy coast, the MTBs managed to creep close inshore, on the landward side of the advancing convoy. The MTBs fired their torpedoes undetected, and Mark Arnold Forster saw his strike a merchant ship amidships and explode.

Then the escort "exploded", and began firing in every direction, but the MTBs managed to slip away at speed, while we distracted and beat up the escort, as we too made our escape, but not before accurate enemy fire had hit us and caused casualties.

It was a classic MTB attack and the next day I attended, with the other Commanding Officers, a Press conference in Dover, and the photograph taken of us at that time appears in Peter Scott's book on pages 120/121.

After the war, Naval Intelligence confirmed that the ship was called *Dalila* (4,000 tons) and was sunk in the attack.

Another particularly memorable occasion was on the night of my 22nd birthday, 4 April 1943.

We set out at dusk for the Belgian coast, Dick Richards in the lead, and supported by ourselves and MGB 117

(Arthur Outen) making up the three boat unit. Once we were across on the other side, we reduced speed on to silent engines, and crept up the swept channel with our rather primitive radar searching the sea ahead.

It must have been around midnight when we detected something near us. We would have communicated with each other by shouting from boat to boat, and Dick would have said "We'll investigate this contact, stand by to attack", and on board, we would tell the gun crews where to expect to see their targets, and we would scan the horizon with our night glasses.

When we eventually made out their dark shapes in the blackness (I can't remember whether there were two or three) we realised they were probably flak trawlers on patrol, and we had surprised them.

As soon as we had got close to them, Dick's boat opened fire on the nearest ship and increased speed, and we all followed suit. The enemy ship took a terrible pounding from our three boats, but the other vessels were now firing accurately at us, but they then turned away and increased speed, leaving our target stopped and burning.

We made another run on our target, and now her guns were no longer firing, and we could hear cries in the water alongside her. Her crew were abandoning her. Dick's voice came across the water, "pick up the survivors, and we will board her, and try and get a tow rope on her".

It is difficult to remember what happened next, but we picked up one survivor from the water, and then went alongside the ship, and Bill and some of our crew jumped on board, and after what seemed ages to me wondering whether we would be attacked in this very vulnerable position, Bill came back with the trawler's signal and code books, and various other trophies.

In the meantime, Dick had decided that the fires on board were so serious that it was unlikely that we could tow the vessel back to Dover, we had our own damage and casualties, and it was best to sink her and return home.

This photograph was found by Bill in a locker on the mess deck of the German ship. It might be of the crew, or of a party ashore, but they all look so young. Were some of them killed or taken prisoner in the action with our boats? You can almost hear the accordion . . .

First of all we took stock of our own position. We had sustained many hits, our front gunner, A/B Jane, was dead, shot through the head, and several others were slightly wounded. There was a large shell hole in the side of the boat, where our petrol tanks were, and a smell of burning, in addition to other damage to the hull and superstructure.

This was when Bill performed a very brave action — he volunteered to hang head down over the side where the shell hole was, and, with an extinguisher, put out any fire there.

So we held him by his legs, until he reported that the tanks did not appear to be holed, and that the hole was well above the water-line.

Dick's voice came across the water, "Our motor mechanic has been aboard the trawler and opened the sea cocks, but she doesn't seem to be filling very fast. We can't leave her in case the enemy comes back, so we must try and sink her with depth charges".

Then 110 dropped a charge as she steamed past the stricken vessel, but it was too far away to do much damage. "113 it's your turn next and you must try and get it underneath her hull."

I knew that the only effective way to do this was literally to go alongside her and drop our charge from a stopped position, and risk being blown up as well, if we didn't get away quickly enough.

We normally envisaged dropping our charges in front of a moving ship, so that the explosion would be underneath, and in order to delay the depth charge pistol (which is operated by water pressure) we had an empty oil barrel on a 50 ft line attached to the charge, to prevent the charge sinking too fast.

This was fine in more normal circumstances, but dropped from a standstill, the wire could get hooked up on a deck fitting or round one of the propellers, when we would be "hoist by our own petard". I therefore cautioned Bill to double check that the line was clear of eveything, and then we slowly proceeded alongside the ship's side, bumped it a number of times, and when we were amidships, I shouted "O.K. Bill", and then, a few seconds later, slammed the throttles open. Bill had done a thorough job — the depth charge didn't follow us, and 113 leapt away like a scalded cat. As we sped away we looked aft, there was an explosion which seemed to lift the trawler slowly up in the air, and then she dropped back, her keel broken, and began to settle quickly.

After a while we started back on the long haul to Ramsgate, exhilarated by our successful action, but suddenly very tired and anxious that it could all have gone wrong, and that we might have been like the wet shivering prisoner on our foredeck, whom we had forgotten in the general excitement.

It was daylight when we reached Ramsgate, and everybody from the other boats, and the base were there to greet us — it had been the successful culmination of a lot of hard training, sea work, and good maintenance of the boats by the crews and base staff, headed by Lieut. Commander Willie Willson, RNVR, that had brought us through.

There was a signal from Vice Admiral Dover saying, "Great work. Regret it was not practicable to bring her back", but we also had the sadness of our crew losses.

Our boat turned out to have more damage than we realised, and it was necessary to take her up to a boatyard, near Twickenham on the River Thames, for a complete refit, and a few days later a tug arrived to tow us round to the Thames estuary, through the centre of London, and to Eel Pie Island, where we paid her off. She had done us very well, but she would fight again under a new crew, with the Polish Navy, and later the Dutch Navy.

After some leave, Bill and I found that we had been appointed to a new 71' 6" MGB No. 121, and we went through the same routine as with 113, going down to Weymouth for a working up period of about six weeks.

It must have been whilst we were at Weymouth that we heard the terrible news that Dick Richards had been lost in an action with German flak trawlers, similar to our own action the month before. Also lost with him was Graham Hughes, my old First Lieutenant.

The loss of this boat and crew hit us very hard, but life, and the war, had to go on.

After Dick was killed, Lieut. R.B. Roper RN, became the Senior Officer of the 9th Flotilla in command of Dick's old boat, 107.

MGB 107 was sunk in March 1944, in an attack on German vessels, between Calais and Boulogne, when she was hit by heavy gunfire, which set her on fire, and Lieut. Roper and all his crew perished.

So in a comparatively short time, of the eight boats

which originally formed the 9th Flotilla, 107 and 110 were sunk in action, with heavy casualties, 113 was paid off after damage in action, and 109 was destroyed by a German mine and suffered casualties.

Such were the hazards of our war in the Dover Straits.

After our working up period, we learnt that 121 was to join a new flotilla up at Lowestoft, and that our new senior officer was to be Norman Macpherson, another RN Lieutenant, who had come from destroyers.

The Lowestoft base was very different from cosy Ramsgate. It was a busy fishing port with many trawlers based there and at Yarmouth, and there were many more Naval vessels, of all kinds.

However, we knew many of the other boats there — I had spent some time there previously, in Lieut. Horne's Flotilla, and we soon settled in.

One big difference was the distance away of the enemy coast, the coast of Holland. Whilst at Dover and Ramsgate it was some 20–30 miles away, here it was more like 100 miles. To get to the enemy shipping lanes meant a long slog, often wet and cold on a grey sea, particularly in winter, and coming back to a low muddy coastline, instead of the white cliffs of Dover. I found that it had a depressing effect on me.

The only action that I particularly remember was one very dark night in July 1943, when we were going slowly along the Dutch coast with a mixed force of MTBs and MGBs. Suddenly a star shell burst above us, and turned the night into day, and there, about 100 yards away and going in the opposite direction was a German E- or R-boat. He was as surprised as we were, but we were quicker on the draw, and our guns immediately raked him from stem to stern. I don't think he fired back at all — he may have been knocked out, but the star shell went out as quickly as it had burst, and we could see nothing more.

We had run into a small convoy and its escorts, and after a general exchange of fire, we seemed to lose them, but our

MTBs got badly mauled, and one had to be towed home.

I often wonder what happened to that E- or R-boat, did he get home? (Naval Intelligence later confirmed one E-boat badly damaged.)

Whilst up at Lowestoft in the summer of 1943, I was thrilled to hear that I had been awarded the D.S.C. for our part in the sinking of the trawler on my birthday in April, and Dick had been awarded the D.S.O.

Sadly his award was a posthumous one, because he had been killed in action in May.

I attended an Investiture by the King at Buckingham Palace in September 1943, accompanied by my Mother and Father. I felt particularly pleased for them. Later that summer Norman Macpherson told me that he was going to be appointed the First Lieutenant of a new fleet destroyer, at present building at Birkenhead, and would I like to come with him as his No. 2. The new destroyer would probably be stationed in the Mediterranean.

With the winter coming on, and my dislike of the East Coast, the idea was inviting. I had been in Coastal Forces since early 1941 and I felt that I was getting stale, and so it came about that I applied for a transfer to destroyers, which was agreed, also that Bill should take over command of 121.

On 7 October 1943 I went to sea in 121 for the last time. I knew that I was going to miss the excitement and exhilaration of driving a fast MGB. For the last time I opened the throttles fully, and felt the rush of wind in my face, and looked back at the long white wake as we reached 40 knots. Then we throttled back, returned to harbour, and I said "O.K. Bill, she's all yours, good luck".

Inevitably, during my time in destroyers, I lost touch with Coastal Forces and my old comrades in arms, but I now know that Bill acquitted himself well in MGB 121 (later renamed MTB 440) and earned himself a good

D.S.C. on the night of 14/15 February 1944. He was in the unit led by Derek Leaf, who was killed that night, during a successful action with flakships and trawlers.

Before going to Ramsgate, I had been in the same Flotilla at Lowestoft as Derek Leaf and Tom Sadleir, both attractive young men who were good officers and good friends. Now they were both gone, like so many other promising young men who would have led their generation post war, had they lived.

"They gave their tomorrows, for our today."

I remember a wartime Armistice Day, which at that time was always observed on 11th November, with a two minutes' silence at eleven o'clock, in memory of those who had lost their lives in the two world wars.

On this day we were on passage to Dover from Ramsgate, inside the Goodwin Sands, and as 1100 approached, we throttled down, cut the engines, and assembled on the foredeck. It was quiet after the noise of the engines, just a slight slapping of the water under the boat's chines, and a sigh of wind in the rigging, and then we stood to attention and remembered those we had known. Whether we said it out loud or not, I don't remember, but in our hearts were those wonderful words from the Armistice service:

> They shall grow not old, as we that are left grow old. Age shall not weary them, nor the years condemn. At the going down of the sun, and in the morning, we will remember them.

And then we went on to Dover.

Yes, we will always remember them, and, in a different context, I will always remember Bill, the tall, quiet

Australian, whose sense of duty and idealism brought him 12,000 miles from his home, and his wife of one week, to help us roll back the German tide, that had swept Europe, and now threatened England.

After leaving Lowestoft, I went on my destroyer courses, was appointed to HMS *Undaunted*, and some 18 months' later, after a very different but very interesting time, arrived in Sydney in 1945, with the British Pacific Fleet, to make contact again with Bill and his wife.

After the war Bill navigated some of Australia's entries for the prestigious America's Cup and Admiral's Cup yacht races in the post war years, and cruised his own yacht over long distances, from his home on the shores of Sydney Harbour.

He ran his family business of Wine Importers, which had started when one of his French forebears in the mid 19th century, sailing as "supercargo" with wine from Bordeaux to Sydney, stayed on there when he met his future wife.

We remained in contact after the war, because he came often to London, and I to Sydney, on business.

He died of cancer in 1990.

After his death his son, Mark, wrote to me asking for information about his father's Naval life in England, as "Dad was a very modest man, and very quiet about his time in Europe".

This was in keeping with my knowledge of Bill's character, so I felt a duty to Bill to tell Mark what I knew, and so this chapter came to be written for Mark and his family, and around it the present book.

Captured E boat Captain

The Author in cold weather gear
(twin Oerlikon guns on right)

CHAPTER 5

Dick Richards and Others

From **The Times** "In Memoriam" Column:

> *RICHARDS* — In proud and loving memory of my son, Lieut. G.D.K. Richards, DSO, DSC, Royal Navy, of "the Little Ships", who lost his life leading his Flotilla in an engagement between Motor Gun Boats and German "E" Boats off the French coast on the night of May 29, 1943, and to the memory of the Officers and Men who died with him.

Dick Richards became my hero in those days at Ramsgate and Dover. I got to know him well, as I spent a lot of time with him, both at sea and in the Base. He was completely dedicated to the Navy and his job, and was good company into the bargain. He never seemed to get flustered or bad tempered, and he always showed great courage and self control.

As such he was the stimulating leader which we all needed, and we would have done anything for him. His private life never obtruded into his service life.

Dick's second son, Christopher, was born six months after his death, and his wife subsequently remarried.

It was a little world of our own that we lived in, bounded by the sea, our colleagues and crews, our boats, and our enemy. Perhaps it was just as well, as these were very dark days for England, which we probably didn't fully comprehend.

I have written my memories of that time in the previous chapters, but others have also written of their own memories of these actions, and of these people, and in 1945

LT. G. D. K. Richards, D.S.O., D.S.C., R.N.

Lieut. Commander Peter Scott, CH, CBE, DSC and Bar, RNVR, published a book called "The Battle of the Narrow Seas" incorporating these, and I have extracted some of the material in his book, to give a balance and a different point of view of those daring days.

". . . That night was an expensive one for the Germans, for at the same time as Lieut. Gemmel was sinking ships off the coast of Holland, the Dover MTBs were doing great work off the coast of the Pas-de-Calais. By this time enemy activity in the Strait had become greatly reduced. The efforts of our MGBs, although they had harassed and upset it, had not been able to prevent the minelaying programme of the previous autumn, and their mid-Channel minefield was regarded by the Germans as complete. But they realised, nevertheless, that the risk to their coastwise convoys was still great, and so they had substantially reduced the number of ships passing through the Narrows. As usual, those which did pass were surrounded with a massive escort, and the fighting was as fierce as ever, but at this period the MTBs working from Dover were seldom in action more than once a month, and not always so often."

New tactics, too, were being developed, involving the co-operation of Fleet Air Arm Albacores and the heavy-gun batteries on the Kentish shore. How successful these tactics could be is shown by the following account of that same night, told by Lieut. B.C. Ward, DSC, RN, who had lately become Senior Officer, MTBs, at Dover.

On 12 March, 1943, a striking force consisting of MTBs 38 (Lieut. M. Arnold Forster, DSC, RNVR), 35 (Lieut. R. Saunders, DSC, RANVR) and 24 (Lieut. V.F. Clarkson, RNVR) was lying at short notice in Dover Harbour. Ward was the Senior Officer of the Force.

"I had just gone to bed, thinking it was a bit late for anything to happen that night," he writes, "when, at about 1 a.m., the Duty Officer rushed in to say that I was wanted on the telephone by the Operations Room at the Castle. I dashed to the phone, shouting like mad, as I went, for the boats to start main engines, and was told that an enemy merchant vessel had been spotted leaving Boulogne, and that we were to go to sea and intercept it.

"Lieut. B. Easton, DSC, RNVR, of MTB 221, whose boat was at long notice that night, had been woken up by all the noise and implored me to let him come too; if only we could hold on for five minutes he would get his boat ready. He was told that we couldn't wait, but that, if he could catch us up, he could join in the party.

"Our three boats got to sea in very quick time and we proceeded at once up Channel towards Dunkirk. A supporting force of MGBs led by Lieut. G.D.K. Richards, DSC, RN, joined us and we all stopped for ten minutes while Richards and I discussed our tactics. Then we set off again for the interception. The wind was fairly fresh, and with a nasty choppy sea we were all getting miserably wet. The big guns at Dover had opened fire on the convoy and the enemy was replying. The enormous white flashes from both sides of the Strait as the guns went off were difficult to distinguish from the bursting of shells, which take over a minute to arrive at the other side.

"As we approached the convoy we could see starshell being fired, and shortly afterwards tracer at the Fleet Air Arm planes that were already going in to attack. In the light of the enemy's starshell, I suddenly caught sight of the merchant ship and shouted out to Arnold Forster, who was beside me, 'Can you see her, Mark?' Just at that moment, to our intense annoyance, the starshells went out, but that glimpse had given us a good idea of the position of the enemy and we crept ahead at 10 knots to get into a good firing position. 'Tin-hat time,' said someone, and we all put on our tin-hats. At last Mark sighted the main target through his binoculars and I shouted out to the other MTBs, 'Enemy in sight.'

"We continued to close in until we were on the enemy's beam at 700 yards' range, and Mark fired his torpedoes as the target steamed across the sights. Dick Saunders, the next boat in line, had also seen the enemy and fired his torpedoes less than half a minute after us. We were sighted by one of the escorts almost immediately after firing torpedoes and the party started. We disengaged at full speed with considerable fire coming at us. Frank Clarkson in MTB 24 had not seen the target and, although he tried to get closer, he was driven off by the escorts. About forty seconds after Mark had fired there was a beautiful explosion amidships of the merchant vessel and a column of water shot up to a hundred feet. Saunders told me afterwards of his disappointment and rage when he saw his torpedoes running perfectly to hit, only to pass just ahead as Arnold Forster's torpedoes stopped the target before his two arrived.

"Meanwhile Dicky Richards and his gunboats (110 and 113) had gone in at full speed and were attacking the escort, as we had previously arranged. They were most gallantly taking a lot of the enemy's fire off us, but not before all the MTBs had been hit.

" 'Teek' (Lieut. H. Teekman, DSC, RCNVR) was out with us, as he always was when he thought there was likely to be a battle. He shouted up to the bridge from down below, saying there was a fire forward. Sub-Lieut. H.G. Bradley, DSC, RNVR, the First Lieutenant of MTB 38, gathered his fire party and staggered down below to put out the fire. It was pitch dark down there, as the lights had been put out by a shell coming in through the ship's side, and he saw a yellow glow coming from a pile of blankets. The blankets were flung away to disclose that the 'fire' was an ordinary miner's lamp that had fallen down owing to the bouncing of the boat in the rough sea. Its light had been shining up through the blankets which had fallen on top of it. We got back to harbour with three minor casualties and only slight damage. The MGBs had had a very spirited action with the escorts, of which there were about a dozen, and having done their job of diverting the fire of some of the enemy from the MTBs, they retired on receipt of a signal from me, as the enemy was by this time fully awake and the odds were at least twelve against three.

"Barry Easton in 221 had left harbour in very quick time some ten minutes after us, but he was just too late to catch up with us before the action started, and had the mortification of returning to harbour without having taken part. It took a lot of explaining to him on our return that we couldn't have waited a bit longer for him to join up.

"A most excellent dinner was provided for us all on the following evening by the Commanding Officers of the MTBs at a neighbouring base, as the result of a bet, made shortly before, on which flotilla would be the next to sink a ship."

The enemy account, which follows, of the two battles fought that night takes a somewhat different, and for them, more optimistic view of the results achieved. It will be recalled while reading it, that Gemmel's force was not engaged with gunfire, and therefore suffered no casualties whatever, and that Ward's force returned to harbour with only slight damage and three minor casualties.

HEAVY NIGHT FOR OUR PATROL BOATS IN THE CHANNEL
FIVE MTBS SUNK, FOUR SET ON FIRE AND ONE DAMAGED
By War Reporter Hans Mänz-Junkers

"As reported in the High Command communiqué of 13th March, a total of five MTBs was sunk off the Dutch coast and in the Channel by German patrol boats; four more were set on fire and one damaged.

"It was a heavy night for our patrols, with bad visibility and, what is more, the convoy was up against heavy seas. Our patrol-boat crews knew that they had to expect something from Tommy. It was a valuable convoy that had to be escorted through the Channel. Soon the vanguard of the convoy had reached the Channel's narrowest part, at Cap Gris Nez. The wind dropped, the sea calmed down. The look-outs doubled their vigilance. Now the place was reached on which Tommy is wont to focus the fire of his shore batteries. And sure enough, here he was. Fire! Now they all knew where we were. One shell after another burst near our convoy, sending up huge columns of water, followed, sometimes, by a shower of splinters over the boats. And now, flashing up from starboard, the fire of our own batteries, which immediately opened up on the enemy batteries. It was certainly a relief for our patrol-boat crews when the British, handicapped in their firing, lowered the intensity of their salvos and had to let the convoy go.

"'Noise of aircraft astern!' the cry resounded over the deck of the leading boat from the look-out post aft. The noise diminished, then came again. Suddenly the surface of the sea was bathed in glaring light. No bombs were dropped; now our patrol-boat men knew where they were. 'Look out for shadows on all sides,' said the Commander. There were bound to be motor torpedo boats in the vicinity. A few seconds later: 'Shadows ahead' came the cry from the fo'c's'le to the bridge. 'Let go a fan of starshells,' the Commander ordered. But even before the shells lit up the black night, one could hear quite plainly the drone of the motor torpedo boats and gunboats which had lain in ambush here, and which now took up fighting position at high speed.

"When the tracer shells first lit up the scene one could see the long black shapes which were now

69

speeding along parallel to the convoy sending over the first tracers in a running fight. Then came the clatter of our automatic weapons. Ever more starshells lit up the great darkness. Then the leading boat scored the first hit on a passing shape. A flame leaps up. The attacking motor torpedo boats alter course to starboard. There are hits on our boats, and the first wounded. Again a glaring flame leaps up, astern this time, where our other boats are situated. So they are attacking there, too. The convoy leader sees to it that the formation is kept, that the patrol-boats' defensive chain is not broken, but none of the attacking boats had access to our convoy steamers. One shot follows another bursting on the enemy boats trying once more to break through. A huge detonation drowns the inferno of our ships' artillery. A Tommy has received a direct hit, apparently in his ammunition store. Yet one of the attackers has scored a hit. One of our boats has been hit by a torpedo and sunk.

"Soon afterwards there followed another great explosion. Another of the attacking boats trying to break through astern had been hit, blown up by the 8.8 cm, and gone down. 'Load and fire' — that was the slogan of our patrol-boat men. When the convoy had safely arrived at the port of destination, the convoy leader was able to report to his escort division: 'Convoy brought in, two enemy motor torpedo boats sunk, two set on fire. One of our boats sunk, the crew saved. Casualties low.'"

Peter Scott continues —
"Amongst the most brilliant and outstanding leaders in Coastal Forces the name of Lieut. G.D.K. Richards, DSC, RN, one of the greatest of them all, has so far appeared only incidentally in this book. This is perhaps because his highly individual

achievements did not conform to the more usual pattern I have described. They stood alone as an example of originality and thoroughness brought, in combination, to a rare perfection.

For more than two years he had been training his MGB Flotilla, based at Ramsgate, for the specialised fighting of the Dover Strait. His boats had been in action dozens of times, few flotillas had wider experience or more extraordinary adventures, and few were more ably or more courageously led.

Take for example the hectic occasion described by Lieut. M. Bray, RNVR, who was in Richards' boat one night for a minelaying operation. "Having completed our job, the three MGBs were beating a rather hasty retreat from some 'T' Class torpedo boats and E-boats, going pretty fast, and chased by the usual assortment of whizzbangs, tracers and starshells. Dick was worried lest we should lose the other two boats and told me to keep my eye on them. I could see a boat on either quarter, following us in nice station, so I reassured him. Just at that moment the telegraphist passed up a signal from Tom Fuller [Lieut. T. Fuller, RCNVR, Commanding Officer of one of the three MGBs] saying he had engine trouble and required immediate assistance, and giving a position some distance astern. This produced a tricky problem: which of the two boats in station on us was friend and which foe? However, one of them started spouting tracers at us, and after a brief exchange we lost him and turned to look for Tom. Over in the distance was a terrific concentration of fire, all of which seemed to be directed on one spot where we thought we could see a boat. "Poor old Tom," we said, "he's had it. There won't be anything left by the time we get there." The telegraphist interrupted us with another signal from Tom, "Engines O.K. Having lots of fun. Come and join us."

Richards' most usual adversaries were flak trawlers, and the technique he had developed for dealing with them was bold in conception and devastating in effect.

One of his greatest successes in this field, and one which earned him the DSO, was on the night of 4/5 April 1943, when he destroyed a trawler off Nieuport and returned with a load of prisoners.

This was the second time that Richards had returned triumphantly with prisoners on board. Last time it had been an R-boat's crew; this time it was a trawler's. Bray describes how he had only one prisoner in his boat, whom he had rescued from the water, very miserable and cold. "On arrival in harbour, where a large armed guard was waiting, I led my sorry-looking specimen up to the Petty Officer in charge, explaining that he had been soaking wet for five hours and should be fixed up with dry clothes as soon as possible. The Petty Officer did not at first recognise him as one of his charges and proceeded to explain in great detail how if he doubled down to the end of the road, turned right and went into the second office on the left he would find the Master at Arms who would fix him up in a jiffy. When I explained that he couldn't understand a word because he was German, the guard gripped their rifles tightly, surrounded him and marched him off as if he had been Al Capone at least."

On 29 May 1943, Richards' Flotilla was ordered to act in support of a minelaying force led by Lieut. Basil Ward. They were to wait off Gravelines to assist the minelayers if they were molested and to return to harbour on completion of the lay at 3 a.m.

LT. P. G. Lee, D.S.C. and Two Bars, R.N.V.R.

Four MGBs were to take part, though Lieut. Philip Lee, DSC, RNVR, the Commanding Officer of one of them, records that there was some doubt whether repairs to his boat would be completed in time for him to sail.

"Richards wasn't very concerned. 'Three boats will be enough,' he said at dinner, 'but come if you can.' He was never very enthusiastic about operations like this one; it was just a routine job with little prospect of action. All the same, I felt unnaturally keen to go. I have always suspected 'routine jobs' of being the most likely time for the startling to happen. Besides it was a lovely, still warm night; after a winter of cold, wet, protracted flogging across the Channel with very little result, the atmosphere was suddenly poignantly reminiscent of the active summer before. It felt as

73

if the 1943 season was just opening, and I did not want to miss the first shoot."

The repair was completed, and Richards in MGB 110 led his force of four boats to sea at half-past ten in the evening.

"We had only just cut our engines at the patrol position off Gravelines," continues Lee, "and the cocoa was only just warming up when the first signal from Ward's minelaying party came up from the wireless office. He had got nearly up to his lay, to find some ships apparently stopped right in his track, about 5 miles to the east of us. Our four boats were lying very close together, quite still on an undistinguished looking piece of glass-calm sea, with darkness 200 yards away in every direction.

Some shouting, sounding very loud, from bridge to bridge; yes, we'd all had the signal, and were plotting the position given. I went below to look at the chart and smoke a cigarette. I looked at our sailing signal: 'To remain until 0300 then return to harbour.' I looked at my watch: 0115. Then another signal from Ward and the cocoa coming up the hatch from the galley. The enemy ships were still in the same place. Trawler patrol, probably. I thought of Ward watching the unsuspecting enemy stopped between him and his laying position. I thought of Richards in 110's chart-house 20 yards away. He would be rocking a pair of dividers thoughtfully over the chart, one point on our position, the other on the enemy's plotted from Ward's signal; looking at his orders: 'return at 0300.' I remembered his reply to a signal from Dover, the previous summer, ordering him to return: 'Returning via Calais,' and then I felt quite certain there was going to be a lot of fighting soon after three o'clock this night.

"A long time to wait, though, with no light, no

movement, no sound except the high-pitched Morse coming from Ward, waiting, still reporting the enemy obstructing him, and the slight rustle from the chart-house as Midshipman Barlow plotted their position on the chart. 'Still there, sir, — same place.' Then nothing but the occasional lapping of water under the chine and the gunners shifting in their turrets.

"We didn't have to wait until 0300. At half-past two a few green tracers floated across the blackness away to the eastward, and then stopped. Richards' voice, very clear in the still air, called 'Start up'; the boats shuddered in quick succession as the muffled exhaust burst through the water and the little group moved off in line ahead towards the Dunkirk channel.

"We were already a mile nearer to the enemy when Ward's next signal came to the bridge. Determined to attempt his lay before the limiting time, he had moved in on the chance of getting past unobserved, but he had been sighted and engaged, turning skilfully away with his mines to leave the enemy for the gunboats. His signal addressed to Richards was concise and adequate: 'Three trawlers' — implying, it seemed. 'Yours if you want them, old boy.' No doubt about it now, I thought: I shouted to the gunners, telling them what I thought was going to happen, and we all put on our tin-hats. The hours of anticipation, and now the slow deliberateness of our approach, were quite unlike any Coastal Force action I'd ever known. I thought how different it had been, for example, that evening last summer when I had been Richards' First Lieutenant. We had pulled our boat off the slip at six, sailed at eight, engaged R-boats at twenty past nine, and were back in harbour by eleven with a cargo of German prisoners. This was somehow much more cold-blooded. Barlow called up from the chart-house to say we should sight them pretty soon on the starboard side, and immediately the darkness seemed to be filled with darker objects as the eyes strained for Ward's 'three trawlers'.

"Suddenly three of them really *were* there, and the nearest one flashed a Morse lamp at 110. Richards was still answering when we turned in — probably sending a rude message in his mock German, I thought; bluffing the already roused enemy for a few precious seconds. The first manoeuvre was just what we expected, the attack we had been specially exercising, and we had had hours in which to think about it. It should be a copy-book attack.

"The bluff didn't last long. One thin streak of tracer from a machine gun, and then sheets of it — at this stage, thank God, in no particular direction. Richards roared straight at the nearest trawler at 35 knots, the rest of us abreast of him to starboard, all foward guns firing: a sharp turn to port when 100 yards off, broadsides at point-blank range, and the trawler was heavily on fire.

"'Stick to the S.O.,' 'Follow father' — all the slogans of the gunboat pundits came to my mind as I concentrated on the vital job of station-keeping, hanging on to the leader's plume as he turned in a wide circle for a second attack. There were plenty of distractions too; a trawler burning furiously astern; tracer still floating towards us, but not very annoying at this range; the ever-recurring concern for the high-bred engines; for the health of the gunners and their guns. Some reassuring shouts from each turret; just time to send a hand to investigate the damage on the starboard bow, where I had noticed a particularly vivid flash, and to be wanly amused at the precision of the report in unhurried Cockney. ''Ole eighteen inches wide, three foot from the water, sir.' Commendable accuracy, I thought; the crew were evidently enjoying themselves."

At this point the third MGB (Lieut. M. O'Mahoney, RNVR) was forced to haul out of line owing to a stoppage in her principal armament, and this unfortunately caused the last boat to lose contact with the other two. Lieut. R.M. Barge, RNVR, her Commanding Officer, proceeded single-handed to attack the last trawler in the line, which he was able to silence.

While he was doing this Richards and Lee came in again on the two leading trawlers, and this time they closed to even shorter range. The Germans were still firing back briskly.

"I didn't like the flashes which came from 110's hull as the shells hit her," continues Lee, "but she never reduced speed. Nobody noticed the explosion of the shell which hit our mast and spattered four of us with splinters. Running in for the third time, I noticed, with a shock, blood on the bridge and then the quickly rising pain and felt furious that this should happen to me at this moment. The leading trawler, which happened to be right ahead, became the object of all my spite, and in concentrating my attention on her I committed the major blunder of losing touch with the leader on a sharp turn. A few seconds later the trawler blew up with a roar, which was some consolation at the time."

Of the three enemy vessels at this stage, one had blown up, another was stopped and silenced and the third was damaged.

With both her officers and two of her crew seriously wounded, however, Lee realised that his boat was in no condition to continue the action, so he set course for harbour and, dangerously wounded though he was, remained on the bridge until she reached harbour at dawn, an action which very nearly cost him his life.

Meanwhile Richards found Barge, whose stopped and silenced trawler the two MGBs closed in upon, with the intention of boarding. Already survivors could be heard shouting in the water. It was at this moment, when the battle had been in progress for almost an hour, that German reinforcements appeared on the scene.

Six E-boats approached at their best speed from the west, to the assistance of their hard-pressed comrades in the trawlers. Faced with this new development after an hour of action, in which much ammunition had been expended, Richards might well have considered withdrawing, but nothing was farther from his intention, and it was then that he made Nelson's favourite signal: "Engage the enemy more closely."

Straight for the six new-comers went the two MGBs, and a most violent and ferocious battle followed. Richards led down the line, the two boats taking the enemy's full broadside, and although our shooting was good, the MGBs were forced to turn away. On disengaging close together, Barge saw that 110 was taking heavy punishment and she immediately burst into flames. The fire was extinguished, but the next moment she disappeared. Observation was difficult due to severe enemy fire, and Barge turned back to look for her. A group of enemy boats and two burning craft were seen; one no doubt was enemy but the other was probably 110. Close approach being impossible, he waited, and after a fruitless search at dawn, Barge joined O'Mahoney and they returned together.

Survivors from Richard's boat were taken prisoner, but he was not amongst them.

Everybody on the deck of MGB 110 was killed, but there were five survivors below decks, who although wounded were picked up out of the water, became prisoners of war, and eventually returned home after the war.

They were Leading Telegraphist W. Lovell, who had served with Dick Richards for two years. Another Leading Telegraphist, Leading Motor Mechanic R. Oakes (who had only joined the boat a few hours before, when Petty Officer Motor Mechanic J. Wibrin D.S.M. and bar became ill and was put ashore that morning,) Leading Stoker McKenzie and Stoker Turnbull.

Leading Telegraphist W. Lovell was kept in solitary confinement by the Germans for three months.

The German account which follows cannot be regarded as of any historical significance. Not until the official German records are available will the true details be known of the final stages in this gallant action.

D.N.B. in German for Europe. 1.9 pm 30th May, 1943

"Berlin (International Information Bureau): According to the latest reports on the naval engagement off Dunkirk on 29th May, British MTBs suffered a heavy defeat. The latest reports available make it clear that, apart from the news of the sinking of two MTBs already reported, the British lost altogether five MTBs, which were sunk by vessels of the German coastguard service. Apart from these five boats sunk, another two were heavily damaged and left burning, and it may be assumed that these boats were also lost.

"During the engagement one of the enemy boats attempted to ram a German vessel, although the former was in a completely hopeless position. Before she succeeded in doing this, a direct hit was obtained upon her and she blew up. It was possible to rescue some of her crew. Other enemy boats attempted to get out of their desperate positions by use of boarding apparatus. This caused them heavy losses in lives. From this dramatic engagement the German crews and their numerically inferior boats emerged with only small losses, which represents a remarkable tribute to their fighting spirit. All German vessels have meanwhile reached their base."

Borkenau. German Home Service via Luxemburg, in German for Germany. 7.15 p.m. 31st May, 1943.

"Encounter between German coastal units and British MTBs near Dunkirk in the morning of 29th May. Five English MTBs sunk; two more set on fire. Some prisoners taken. No losses on the German side.

"The commander of one of the German E-boat flotillas engaged in the encounter tells his story: 'The whole thing developed so rapidly that the English were as surprised as ourselves. Certainly two English boats found themselves at 20 metres from us and were so flabbergasted that at first they forgot to fire. We blazed away as best we could and the English, who in amazement sailed across our whole front-line, got hits from one of our boats after another. The two boats caught fire quickly and one sank. The other veered round sharply and disappeared in flames. Shortly afterwards I saw something burning in the distance, and guessed it was one more MTB. I moved near, attempting to encircle it. But when my circle was starting to form two more English boats broke into it, firing in all directions and getting fire from all sides. One of the boats broke through my ring, and a fight at close quarters ensued. Hand grenades were thrown; that boat also started to burn and disappeared in flames. The other boat could not break through, and finally, as a last resort, attempted to ram one of my boats. But it got very heavy fire from that boat and from another one near by, and just before it could ram there was an explosion. Its magazine was blown up; it caught fire and sank. We succeeded in saving five survivors and took them with us. We ourselves went safely back into harbour.'"

It seems that the two British boats made their presence felt.

Many tributes have been paid to Richards' brilliant leadership. His determination, his sheer courage and, above all, his enthusiasm were of the order which constitutes greatness.

"Life was one huge adventure for him," wrote one of the officers of his Flotilla. "He never got flustered and, even at sea, regarded everything as highly amusing. I can remember one night in the summer of 1942, sitting beside him on the bridge whilst we crept about, rather too near the French coast, looking for shipping. Dick was enjoying every moment of it, singing *Sur le pont d'Avignon* and suggesting mad schemes. He ought to have lived in the days of Drake."

Ronnie Barge wrote recently:—

"Dick Richards was a character. I knew him very well and liked him.

"I think that his personality is well described by various remarks by others in Peter Scott's "Battle of the Narrow Seas".

"He was certainly brave, but apt to be foolhardy. On several occasions, I had to restrain him from drawing us all into extraordinary unauthorized operations — commando style — on the French coast.

"I, speaking some German, was to board a German ship posing as a French harbour official! Meantime, others were to be preparing to sink the ship — good fun!

"He was colourful and no-one could help liking him. He certainly *was* a leader."

Derek Leaf and Tom Sadleir

The month of July began with a lively attack on an enemy convoy. This time Lieut. P.A.R. Thompson, DSC, RCNVR, who had taken part in the destruction of the E-boat in March, led three of the old 70-foot MGBs in to engage three escorted merchantmen — one of them a tanker — off the Dutch coast.

The Commanding Officers of the other two boats were Lieut. M.T.C. Sadleir, RNVR, and Lieut. E.D.W. Leaf, DSC, RNVR. It was the first time that this Flotilla, which was primarily concerned with hunting E-boats, had become involved with an enemy convoy, and it is clear that Pete Thompson (later a prisoner of war after his capture in the Straits of Messina) was not going to let the chance of an offensive action pass him by.

Leaf wrote a spirited account of the battle, admirably illustrated, in his diary:

"It was a thundery summer night. Pouring rain and pitch darkness one moment and five minutes later a clear sky with bright moonlight illuminating the clouds around us. We were creeping down the coast during one of the bright intervals when a bright, hostile-looking white light

LT. E. D. W. Leaf, D.S.C. and Bar, R.N.V.R.

challenged us. We turned to investigate it. Dark
shapes appeared up moon — E-boats? No! E-boats
don't carry balloons! This is probably one of those
convoys we read about which the aircraft of Coastal

Command often attack. [The passage which follows
is a facsimile extract from Lieut. Leaf's diary.]

No time to speculate — what is Pete, the leader, going to
do? Crikey! He's going in to attack! O lord! What with? We have no torpedoes
only two depth charges. This should be interesting. This is what it looked
like to me though of course it was really very/darker — thank goodness:—

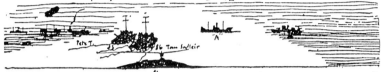

We approached up-moon and made for the gap. Suddenly, as if we had all
finally made up our minds we increased speed and waited for what was
bound to come. Nearer and nearer ..... Fizz! A starshell right over our
bows then it came. We were travelling by then and we had spread out.

"It was marvellous how we got through — the
shooting was plentiful but not quite good enough;
perhaps we were not expected. A lot of the stuff was
going over our heads. I was fascinated by one ship
on my port beam which looked just like a giant
catherine wheel on Guy Fawkes night. Something
made me look ahead again, and it was just as well,
for we were steering straight for one of the
merchants ships ('A' in the picture).

"My point-five gunners were concentrating on its
bridge and a few sparks were flying off it. We had
to go hard a-port to avoid ramming her, and I just
remembered to pull the string which drops the
depth charges. The first did not go, but the second
went all right. I could see the name on her bow, but
it somehow did not stay in my memory — at the
time it seemed rather like some French word like
Aiglon; perhaps it will come back to me one day.
For ages, it seemed, the charge did not go off, then I

84

Derek Leaf and Tom Sadleir were two of the CO's in the 7th MGB
Flotilla

felt a bump, and simultaneously the escort vessel
'B' opened fire, to which we replied. I could see Pete
and Tom ahead, but I did not look round to see the
effect of our attack. The Oerlikon gunner saw it go
off abreast her foremast, so it probably strained her
a bit. Later we looked back and saw a good deal of
shooting going on at random in the convoy. They
did chase us for a bit, using starshells, but we got
away. One man was wounded, and so was Pete in
83; apart from that the boats were unscathed
except for a few odd bullet- and small shell-holes.
We returned just before breakfast, and were we
dehydrated!"

Later in the month depth charges were used
again against German shipping off the coast of
Holland, this time by Lieut. Commander G.E.
Bailey, RNVR.

Since Jermain first worked it out in the winter of
1940, the depth-charge technique had rarely been
used against surface ships. Because of the very
short distance ahead of the enemy at which the
depth charges must be laid, this type of attack is
the most hazardous of all. Each opportunity that

arose called for outstanding determination in crossing the enemy's track only a few yards from his bows.

For a dashing attack under the bows of a trawler, in which his boat was riddled with gunfire and only one of his crew remained unwounded, Lieut. Commander Bailey won the Distinguished Service Order. [He was killed two years later in July, 1944, when the ship in which he was serving was torpedoed by E-boats north of Le Havre, during the early stages of the invasion of Normandy.]

By the beginning of 1944 some of the E-boats had been rearmed, and they began to show a more offensive spirit. It was for the time being short lived, as we shall see, but although their operations against our convoys were crowned with less and less success, a hitherto almost unknown phenomenon made its appearance one night in February. E-boats deliberately sought contact with our Coastal Forces.

When they made a sortie against our east-coast route on the night of 14/15 February, they were driven off by our destroyers without interfering with our convoys. As they withdrew, two units of Coastal Force craft were racing to a point in mid-Channel to cut off their retreat. The Senior Officer of these boats was Lieut. E.D.W. Leaf, DSC, RNVR, and when he reached the prescribed position in the vicinity of Brown Ridge he felt sure that the E-boats were already ahead of him; but he was not to be cheated of action. At once he decided to push on towards Ijmuiden and wait on the doorstep for the returning Germans, a decision which the Commander-in-Chief, Nore, described in the report to Admiralty as "entirely correct".

As Leaf approached the Dutch coast he came upon a defence patrol consisting of a medium-sized flakship and two trawlers, and he made up his mind at once to attack, putting into operation a prearranged plan. In his force he had five seventy-one-foot-six boats, one of which was fitted with torpedo tubes. This boat was detached to attack with torpedoes while the four gunboats went in to draw the enemy's fire. It was the old combined attack, only on a smaller scale, and it was entirely successful. Both MTB 455's torpedoes hit the target, and a few moments later her guns scored hits on the leading trawler, while Leaf engaged the rear trawler at 100 yards and left it silenced and burning. When the shore batteries joined in our force withdrew to re-form, reload and attack again. As they did so, steering north-west at high speed, they ran straight towards another enemy ship which they did not see until the range was very short. Leaf's boat was heavily hit and suffered serious casualties. The rest of the force made answer as they went past, apparently to good effect, but it was too late to save their leader. Leaf himself and three ratings had been killed and two others wounded.

It was 4.15 when the force re-formed. Neither the damaged boat nor 455 were in company, but Lieut. C.A. Burk, RCNVR, immediately took charge of the rest of the Unit — three boats — and set off to look for Leaf. Almost at once a party of six E-boats was detected shadowing on the port quarter and gradually closing in. Two more groups of E-boats were detected ahead, and so Burk decided to tackle the first lot first. He turned hard a-port at full speed and crossed ahead of the E-boats at a range of 100 yards — a manoeuvre known as crossing the enemy's T. As each of our boats passed ahead of the enemy line with all guns firing, only the forward gun of the foremost E-boat could fire in return. As a result, the first two E-boats were hard hit, and the leader turned to port, ceased fire and stopped, with a fire burning aft. Unfortunately the last of our boats lost touch during this action, but the other two sighted the next group of E-boats, six more, closing from right ahead. Once more Burk led across the enemy's T, and once more the first two E-boats suffered. The MGBs were heavily outnumbered, and now broke off the engagement to the westward, meeting two more E-boat groups and engaging each as it passed. These two boats had been in action against no fewer than seventeen E-boats, yet Burk's boat had sustained no casualties or damage, and the second in his line had only three men slightly wounded.

"During last night," said the Germans on their radio, "German E-boats, in spite of enemy destroyer attacks, carried through an operation off the English coast according to plan and without loss. At the same time German outposts off the Dutch port of Ijmuiden intercepted British light coastal craft, sank three of these vessels in a fierce engagement and forced the others to turn away. The returning E-boats attacked this battered enemy formation, by their fire destroyed another two boats and damaged several others. The enemy suffered heavy casualties. All our boats returned to their bases; damage to them was slight."

So once again out of a force of five boats the enemy claimed to have sunk them all and damaged several more, and it is hard to believe that a medium-sized flakship could survive two torpedo hits. Leaf's force had certainly made its presence felt. But the loss of so brilliant and dashing a leader was indeed a setback. Derek Leaf had already achieved so much since the early days of which he wrote in his diary. How much more could he not have achieved, had there been time? It has been written of him that "boyhood shone in his face after manhood came, as loath to 'fade into the light of common day'; and his courage was the untroubled courage of a boy. If events furnished no occasion for daring, he would make them for himself in manoeuvring his ship; and in action and out he chose the most aggressive course, and reduced caution to its irreducible minimum. His fire-eating so impressed the lower deck that, it is said, superstitious sailormen would cross themselves as they passed his ship, for luck for him and for themselves. He served in the spirit of the greatest sailor of all, and died, like him, conscious of victory."

Less than three weeks later the German reaction to the combined MGB/MTB attack had begun to make itself felt. On 30 September, Dickens led another such attack, with MGBs under Lieut. J.S. Dyer, RN. Once again Perkins showed his outstanding marksmanship in firing torpedoes. Two torpedo hits are believed to have been scored, but the battle was fierce and there were a number of casualties on our side. Amongst them Lieut. M.T.C. Sadleir, RNVR, was killed instantly on the bridge of his boat. As usual, the German claim was over-optimistic. In their broadcast two days later they admitted that one of their patrol boats had sunk, but they claimed that no fewer than four of our boats had been destroyed and two others damaged. On the following day a long account of the battle was broadcast in support of this somewhat fantastic claim.

The loss of Tommy Sadleir was a great blow to his Flotilla and to the base at Lowestoft. He was typical of the eager and vigorous men who commanded the MGBs and fought night after night to maintain their initiative in the North Sea. The strain of this fighting is well described in a passage written of Sadleir by his father, Michael Sadleir, the novelist [this passage is taken from a privately printed memoir]:

"On his last two leaves, when he was sitting alone with me and reading, or thought himself unobserved, he would sink into a sort of wistful brooding, and I feared that he was thinking of the many responsibilities of his command and of the danger and exhaustion of what for him and his friends had become the whole of existence. No outsider could intrude on a private unhappiness of this sort, nor could an ignorant civilian do more than guess at the strain under which the young men of the light coastal forces — for all the gaiety, comradeship and excitement of their job — were forced to live. One could only try to make the fleeting period of his leave fill the foreground of his thoughts, and so gain for him a short respite from the cruel apprehension laid on a whole generation of young people by a handful of evil men."

From all these accounts it might be thought that our boats were manned by Officers only, which would be very far from the truth.

Each boat was a tightly knit team of young men working together.

After the Commanding Officer and First Lieutenant, came the Coxswain (usually a Petty Officer) who was in charge of the crew. Each main gun had a gunner and his mate, who was responsible for reloading in action. The forward gun crew were particularly exposed on the foredeck to wind and spray, and in winter in the North Sea, must have had a very uncomfortable time. Less so the after gun turret.

The Coxswain steered the boat from the bridge, alongside the Commanding Officer, and the First Lieutenant had the protection of the wheelhouse for his navigation.

Also comparatively warm and sheltered was the radio operator, below decks.

Almost the worst place in the boat at sea was the engine room. There was only crouching headroom for the motor mechanic and his mate, and the noise from the three big Packards was indescribable. Speech was impossible, and the engine room crew had no knowledge of what was happening or where we were — they just worked to keep the engines going. They were all unsung heroes.

Yet, like submariners, they preferred being in small boats, rather than larger vessels with more facilities but greater discipline and restrictions.

They got extra "hard lying" money, and like submariners wore white jerseys instead of the usual uniform.

And what happened to some of these young men who survived the Battle of the Narrow Seas?

Peter Liddell, DSC, commanded an MTB, and after the Normandy Invasion, with others, had a very busy time in the Channel, attacking shipping which was trying to support the resistance of the German Army on the North French coast to the advancing Allies.

Rodney Sykes, DSC, commanded an MTB at Felixstowe and later, in the Channel. After the war (despite the petrol incident!) he became a respectable partner in a big firm of Stockbrokers in the City, and the Master of the Vintners Company.

Ronnie Barge, DSC, continued his distinguished service with MGBs, and after the war returned to his native Clyde, married and had a large family, and worked for a Glasgow Shipping Company. He painted for me the wonderful picture of MTBs operating at night. See page no. 25. He pioneered salmon farming in Scotland.

Mark Arnold Forster, DSO, DSC, joined the editorial staff of the Manchester Guardian, and became a well known contributor to that respected paper, and to the Observer. He wrote a book called "The World at War" which was made into a television serial. He died comparatively young.

David James, DSC, commanded an MGB in Hichen's Flotilla at Felixstowe. His boat was sunk in action off the Dutch coast. Hichens went back to pick up the survivors, some of whom he got on board, but David was on the end of a rope when the enemy boats opened fire again, and Hichens had to leave him behind, to prevent further casualties. He was taken prisoner, and eventually escaped to Sweden at his second attempt, and got back to England. He wrote a book about his exploits, and after the war became a Tory Member of Parliament.

Philip Lee, DSC. Sadly I lost touch with him, but I know that he died after the war.

Ronnie Carr, DSC. After the war he put his considerable artistic talents to work in the interior decorating world. He designed furniture and hand painted objects, and he could draw and paint pictures and portraits beautifully. We kept in touch with him, mainly through Rodney Sykes, and he died in 1992. He left a widow and four children.

Corny Burke, DSC, Tom Ladner, DSC, and Doug Maitland, DSC, all Canadians from Vancouver, became known as the "Three Musketeers", when they were all Commanding Officers of the bigger "D" class MGBs, working together in the Mediterranean, with conspicuous success.

Their success continued into their post war lives, and I am told that every few years they meet, together with others of their old colleagues, for a reunion in some of the places where they were based and fought, in the Italian campaign.

Tom Fuller DSC. This colourful Canadian character, who was older than most of us, had a good war in the Channel, and in the Mediterranian, in D class boats, and afterwards built up a successful International Civil Engineering Company based in Canada.

Douglas Hunt, DSC. After the war, in his spare time, he founded the MTB Officers' Association, and has since organised forty-five annual reunions in London, which have been a most valuable means of keeping people in touch. He also arranges for the Members of the Association to attend the Annual Armistice Day Memorial Service at HMS *Hornet*, the MTB Base at Portsmouth, when wreaths are laid by representatives of Naval Organisations from many countries.

HMS *Undaunted* in the Pacific – Fleet Carriers in distance

CHAPTER 6

H.M.S. UNDAUNTED

My destroyer courses lasted about six weeks and took place in various locations according to the subject, from torpedoes up in Dunoon in Scotland to gunnery at Whale Island in Portsmouth.

Also on my course I was delighted to find Ronnie Carr, who had been a Commanding Officer in Felixstowe in one of the flotillas. He was a very civilised person, artistic and rather like Ronnie Barge from Ramsgate. It was therefore an enjoyable period apart from being interesting.

Another member of our course was a Lieut. Nicholas Monserrat. He was a quiet man who didn't mix very much with us, and of course at that time he had not written "The Cruel Sea" and become an internationally famous author as he did after the war.

After my courses I was sent up to Birkenhead where the *Undaunted* was building at the yard of Cammell Laird and was due to be completed in about two months' time. Norman Macpherson was already there, together with the Engineer Officer, and we all lived in a rather uncomfortable pub round the corner from the yard.

Our job was to familiarise ourselves with the equipment and layout of the ship and there wasn't really a great deal to do. I found Birkenhead and across the river, Liverpool, pretty depressing places.

Also building at the yard at the same time was a submarine called *Stygian* and we soon became friends with the First Lieutenant, Hugh Somerville. Our own Commanding Officer, Lieut. Commander Angus

Mackenzie, was also there and so we had an opportunity to get to know him. He was from the Merchant Service and was an aggressive Scotsman. He used to play the bagpipes and his big interest in life was fishing, and later on when we were up in Scapa Flow, he used to go off in the ship's boat endlessly, and keep his supply of worms for fishing in the wardroom bath.

Gradually the other officers and ratings joined the ship, there was another RNVR Lieutenant, Michael Potter, and the Navigator Jonathan Huntingford who was a very bright RN officer with whom I shared a cabin in the after part of the ship. There was also another RNVR Lieutenant and a Ship's Doctor and the Gunnery Officer "Guns".

Undaunted was a Fleet destroyer with four 4.7 inch guns, 8 torpedoes, and a miscellaneous collection of 40 mm and 20 mm anti-aircraft guns. Two flotillas of these destroyers were built and our flotilla leader was *Grenville*, otherwise they all had names beginning with "U". There were about 10 officers and a crew of 180 ratings.

They were driven by oil-fired steam turbines, with a speed of about 32 knots.

A Fleet destroyer was one which worked with the Fleet in an offensive role, as compared with an Escort destroyer or Frigate, which had a defensive role escorting convoys, etc. As a Fleet destroyer, we thought that we were a cut above the others!

I was to be a Watchkeeping Officer, and the Fo'c'sle Officer, which meant that I was in charge of the upper deck forward, when we were anchoring or coming into harbour, or picking up a mooring buoy. At action stations I was in charge of the anti-aircraft guns amidships, and I was also responsible for firing the torpedoes if we ever made a torpedo attack. In this case I was on the bridge where the torpedo sights were located. I was also put in charge of the Ship's Office, a duty which I did not take to, but I had a very good Writer who in fact did all the detail work.

On the Bridge of HMS *Undaunted*

Once we were in commission we joined the other ships of our Flotilla up at Scapa Flow in order to work up the ship and also to do flotilla exercises.

Scapa Flow had been the main Fleet base in the 1914–18 war and is a vast area of protected water surrounded by small islands, very uninhabited, to the north of Scotland in the Orkney Islands. It could accommodate a huge number of ships and once you were there you might just as well have been at sea except that the ship was still.

A grim reminder of the war was the wreck of the battleship Royal Oak which had been torpedoed by the Germans in the early part of the war with the loss of hundreds of her crew. She sat on the bottom with her funnels and masts sticking up out of the water.

Whilst there we fired our guns at surface targets, fired our guns at aircraft targets, and for the first and only time in my life we fired the torpedoes.

97

We had eight 21 inch torpedoes mounted amidships in
two ~~turrets~~ which were normally trained fore and aft, but
when one came to fire them they could be trained out on
either beam. The torpedoes were powered by compressed
air which was contained in cylinders in the body of the
torpedo, and they had a very intricate and marvellous
control system which steered them in a straight line and
at a depth which had been set on the torpedo before firing,
and they had a large warhead full of TNT on the front end
which was sufficient to sink a large ship if it was hit.
When the torpedoes were fired they would be blown out of
the tubes by a small charge of cordite and would hit the
water with their engines and control system running, and
they would then travel at about 45 knots until the air ran
out in about five or six miles.

In a torpedo attack my job was, when the target had
been identified, to calculate by eye and guesswork the
course and speed of the target ship and set this on the
sight at the side of the bridge, instruct the torpedo crews
on which side the ~~turrets~~ were to be trained, and when the
Captain began the attack he would have to slowly swing
the ship round so that the target came on the beam, and I
would give the order to fire each torpedo individually as
my sights came on to the target ship. If all eight torpedoes
were fired, then they would go out in the shape of a fan,
and this spread should give a good chance of at least one of
them hitting the target.

I was always amazed that this very sophisticated
weapon, with its own crew who spent a lot of time
maintaining them, was in those days finally dependent on
this very crude torpedo sight on the side of the bridge.

Luckily we never had to fire our torpedoes in anger.

Scapa Flow is a cold and windy place at the best of times,
and of course in the winter it was pretty unpleasant.
Coming into harbour as Fo'c'sle Officer I had to stand to
attention right up in the bow of the ship with the fo'c'sle
party lined up on either side until we were ready to start

picking up our mooring buoy.

First the anchor chain had to be disconnected from the anchor, and then sufficient chain run out so that it could be connected to the buoy, which was a very large steel round floating platform, and it was the Captain's job to bring the ship up into the wind so that the buoy was just under the bow, so that one of the fo'c'sle party could jump down on to it and connect the chain to the ring of the buoy.

This was quite a performance, especially when we were new to it and the final act of putting the pin in the shackle attached to the ring of the mooring buoy was completed by putting a lead pellet into a hole in the side of the shackle. If the sea was rough this could be quite a difficult job and in one of our earlier attempts, the pin was dropped over the side and it was then discovered that we had not got another one on board. The Captain was not best pleased.

Whilst the sea in the Flow was reasonably calm, it was not calm once one got outside the anchorage, and in fact this is one of the roughest seas around the United Kingdom and there are always strong winds.

Going to sea after some days in harbour was often a trial as we had lost our "sea legs" and as soon as we started pitching and rolling a lot of people including myself were afflicted with seasickness for at least 24 hours.

One of the exits from the Flow was past an amazing "stack" called the Old Man of Hoy. It is a vertical rock, about 600 feet high, and it was always particularly nice to pass it going the other way into the Flow and comparatively calm waters.

One day we were ominously supplied with cold weather gear which consisted of windproof fur-lined trousers and tops, and we knew then that we were going to be sent to the North. We were to escort a force of carriers and battleships which were backing up a Russian convoy setting off to Murmansk, and we accompanied them up off the Norwegian coast.

These convoys were savagely attacked by German

aircraft and also threatened by their battleships which were stationed in some of the Norwegian fjords, and some of these convoys sustained very heavy losses, supplying the Russians with much needed equipment. It was not a pleasant job and one knew that if we were sunk and survived in the water, we would probably only survive for a further two or three minutes because of the cold.

On these operations we would be closed up at action stations for a lot of the time, and also in two watches, which meant that we had four hours on deck and four hours off throughout the day and night.

It was quite a responsibility to be the Officer of the Watch, frequently alone in charge of the ship, but the Captain would be in his sea cabin just below, and could always be called upon if necessary. One had to keep in station on the other ships of the fleet, which meant that your position had to be on a certain bearing at a certain distance, and you had to manoeuvre the ship to keep there both day and night. At night you could either do this by sight if it was a clear night or by radar if it wasn't. It became more complicated when the fleet manoeuvred and signals would be sent by flashing light or by radio, and the fleet usually travelled fast so as to reduce the danger from U-boats.

For the same reason, both the convoy and the fleet would carry out a zigzag course. This meant that at certain times of the hour the course would be altered so many degrees to either port or starboard, and the new course was maintained until it was time to make the next turn. These zigzags were numbered and one could then look them up in a manual and see exactly what time of the hour the course was changed and how many degrees it would be to port or starboard, and you had to automatically carry this out, once the Commodore of the convoy or the fleet had decided which number zigzag they would use. To help the Officer of the Watch there was a zigzag clock on the bridge which could be set to sound a bell whenever an alteration

From back of Bridge of *Undaunted*. Destroyers in line ahead, in rough sea

was due.

This zigzagging was very effective because a U-boat trying to get into position to attack, would suddenly find that his target altered course twenty or thirty degrees either way, and he was then in the wrong position.

I had a young Canadian Sub-Lieutenant in my watch, who also lived aft, and one rough night he failed to come on watch. He suffered badly from seasickness and it can only be assumed that coming forward, and weakened by seasickness, he was swept overboard.

It was nice to be back in Scapa Flow again after these Russian convoys, and to go ashore on one of the barren islands and stretch one's legs. On one of these islands was a Church of Scotland hut, manned by ladies who came from somewhere, and who provided tea. This was about the only shore facility that there was, although there was a destroyer depot ship, HMS *Tyne*, which carried stores and other facilities for us.

101

This lack of shore facilities for the Navy may have been the reason for the probably apocryphal story of the stoker from HMS *Rodney*, who was caught having "unnatural relations" with a sheep.

His defence, that "he thought it was a Wren in a duffle coat", was not accepted!

I think that we had films on board, but one red letter day we were visited by a small ENSA party, which consisted of John Mills and his wife and Bernard Miles and his wife and two or three supporting cast. John Mills had recently made the film "In Which We Serve" about destroyers, and so he was very interested to come on board and go right round the ship.

They gave us a very amusing hour or more of entertainment which was good for our morale. (By an extraordinary coincidence, when I was living in Hampshire in the 1970s, we got to know a very nice couple who lived near us, and the wife was an actress who started talking about her experiences one day. It turned out that she had been, as a young girl, with this ENSA team, and must have been one of the people on board the ship with us).

During this period at Scapa Flow we were joined by an army officer, whose job was gunnery liaison. We didn't know it at the time, but this was part of the lead up to and preparations for the Normandy landings, because his job was to go ashore with a radio, and in communication with us, guide our guns on to shore targets which we couldn't necessarily see. We therefore practised this new idea using some of the uninhabited islands.

He was a very nice man but could not pronounce his "r"s and his name was Remington Hobbs, and he used to say "You can always remember my name as Typewiter Cwicketer". He stayed with us until on D-day, off the Normandy beaches, he went ashore with the troops and directed our guns at German targets.

That spring the Flotilla was ordered down to the south

coast of England where the invasion fleet was being assembled in all the various harbours along the south coast and primarily in the Solent. Our Flotilla was to anchor off Yarmouth in the Isle of Wight, an area which I knew well from my sailing days as a boy. It was an amazing sight, ships everywhere, and a sense of excitement and foreboding as we realised that this was the invasion fleet to take the Allied armies back into France.

The scale of the operation and the organisation behind it was quite incredible and a few days before D-day we were given our confidential briefing of our role.

We were to cross over before the landing craft and arrive at our station off the coast at dawn, where we were to anchor, just off the shore, and to engage with our guns specified targets such as gun emplacements on the beach, which would have hindered our troops landing. We were given very detailed photographs of our stretch of shoreline taken at wave top height by Spitfires with cameras in their wings and each of our targets was numbered and clearly identified. To seaward of us would be the cruisers and bigger ships which would engage the German shore batteries with their bigger guns. Once the naval force had accomplished their job, the landing craft would come through and land their troops. It sounded very hazardous for us.

There were several days to go before D-day, and I remember going ashore at Yarmouth and walking up the little lanes behind the town, which were fresh and green with spring flowers and foliage, the English countryside at its best. I remember wondering whether I would see it again.

The day before we were due to leave, the weather suddenly went bad, it blew a gale, and everybody became very worried. Then a patrol vessel with a loud hailer ran through the lines of ships broadcasting the message that Operation Overlord was postponed for 24 hours. It was a considerable anticlimax.

However, the next day the weather had improved and that evening we hauled up our anchor and slipped out through the Needles channel and set course for France at slow speed.

I remember that it was a quiet night, and rather than try and catch a few hours' sleep in my cabin aft, I stayed on deck and sat with my back to the superstructure, just above the fo'c'sle break, watching the sea go by, and wondering what was awaiting us.

In the early hours we closed up at action stations, and noticed a lot of air activity over the Cherbourg peninsula, which was drawing anti-aircraft fire from the Germans. This was the initial parachute force going in to drop behind the lines, together with the troop-filled gliders towed by their aircraft tugs. Ahead of us was the French coast but it was all quiet.

As the sky began to lighten in the east, we slipped into our position off our beach in the Bay of the Seine, and I was sent forward to anchor the ship. We must have been spotted by the Germans at this time, because there were gun flashes behind the coast and then shells began to drop around us. I felt very naked up on the fo'c'sle.

It was getting light by now and we could see our targets just as they were shown in the photographs that we had been given, and immediately we started firing our main armament at our targets on the beach and cliffs. Luckily the cruisers to seaward of us had also started to fire at the shore batteries which were shelling us, and in a short while they had been silenced and were no longer worrying us.

It was then that hundreds of landing craft appeared from seaward, and passing us, their troops waving, they beached themselves on the sand, and the troops were able to get ashore without too many casualties and establish themselves.

Initially there were some air attacks on the fleet and the beaches, but after a bit our own aircraft seemed to get

control of the air and we were not unduly molested.
"Footprints in Time", by Sir John Colville, gives a vivid account of how he saw the invasion fleet from his fighter plane.

"At 3.00 a.m. I was awoken for briefing. The skies had cleared and in the early light I set off with one accompanying aircraft to perform a tactical reconnaissance of an area in Normandy near Falaise. As we set course for Selsey Bill, flying over the somnolent Hampshire villages and fields flecked by the rising sun, it was impossible not to feel exultantly melodramatic and I doubt if I was the only pilot that morning who told himself with commonplace self-satisfaction that 'Gentlemen in England, now a-bed, shall think themselves accursed they were not here, and hold their manhood cheap ...' I even wished it were St Crispin's Day.

"The Channel was teeming with ships: convoys of landing craft, large and small; big troop-ships; destroyers and cruisers: thousands of ships with their white bow-waves and thousands of barrage balloons. In the sky we mingled with an equally vast array of Spitfires and Typhoons of the RAF and Lightnings and Thunderbolts of the US Army Air Force. We were in the van of the greatest Crusade of all times, elated to the extent of spiritual intoxication, and so instilled with a sense of unity with those thousands of others who were setting forth on the same venture that the hazards ahead were of no consequence, and fear was a forgotten emotion. War in these conditions is, for a short span, magnificent.

"A long line of men-of-war lay off the Normandy coast, their big naval guns blazing and the burst of their shells inland distinctly visible. The trajectory

105

of their missiles was high and that very morning one of my brother officers in 168 Squadron was struck by a 15″ shell from the Warspite, he and his plane entirely disintegrating. The chances of being hit by a 15″ shell when flying at 5000 feet must be small indeed."

All through that amazing day waves of landing craft continued to arrive, our Gunnery Liaison Officer, Captain Remington Hobbs, went ashore and we were able to support the advancing troops with our gunfire directed by him. There were also some amazing sights as the concrete sections of the Mulberry harbours began to arrive, towed by tugs and put into position, and later on an extraordinary contraption called PLUTO (Pipe Line under the Ocean) which were huge floating drums of hosepipe, towed by tugs, which were unrolling miles of petrol hose across the Channel and were the means of supply of petrol to the army when they got ashore.

By the evening things were comparatively quiet in our sector as the batteries and coastal defences had been silenced and the troops had been able to advance several miles inland, and there wasn't much enemy air activity. Luckily we were all on a considerable "high", so that exhaustion hadn't caught up with us and we were able to go back to a two-watch system and get some food and rest.

The next day (D+1), we proceeded westward parallel to the beach, to see what was going on, when we were suddenly hailed by one of the Navy's fast minelayers, HMS *Apollo*. She called us up on her lamp to say that unfortunately she had run aground, and she had on board some VIPs, who had to be taken back to Portsmouth, and we were to take them on board.

We were surprised and delighted to find that the VIPs were General Eisenhower, the Commander in Chief of the whole operation and Admiral Ramsay who was the Commander in Chief of All Naval Forces, together with

General D. Eisenhower comes aboard *Undaunted* from HMS
Apollo, off Normandy beaches on D + 1
Capt. Remington Hobbs and Lieut. N. MacPherson on right

Admiral Sir Bertram Ramsay comes aboard

their staffs. They had been reconnoitring the beachhead on board *Apollo* when unfortunately she hit a sandbank and lost a propeller.

They came on board and had a quick glass of sherry in the wardroom and then went up to the bridge when we set course for Portsmouth at high speed.

As soon as we discovered who we had on board, we had to make a Five Star General's flag and hoist it to the masthead as we steamed through the fleet, which was very satisfactory as every ship that we passed and which we would normally have had to salute as they were senior to us, now had to salute us. General Eisenhower was very nice and friendly and spoke to everyone, and was able to tell us that the landing was going well, and we duly put them all ashore in Portsmouth Harbour.

By chance last year I read an obituary in the Daily Telegraph of a Captain J. Grindle, who had been the Captain of the *Apollo* at the time, and must have had a most ghastly experience when he ran his ship aground. The obituary contained a reference to this incident and the relevant portion is as follows:

"Captain John Grindle, who has died aged 90, successfully overcame one of the most unfortunate mishaps ever to befall a naval officer.

"In 1944 he took command of *Apollo*, a brand new 40-knot minelayer, and was mentioned in despatches for the ship's part in laying defensive minefields in the English Channel in April and May 1944 to guard the Normandy assault area against U-boats.

"But on D-Day plus-one, June 7, the ship left Portsmouth for a tour of inspection of the Normandy beaches, having embarked a party that included the Supreme Allied Commander, Gen. Eisenhower, and the Allied Naval Commander, Adml. Sir Bertram Ramsay, together with members of their staffs.

"Off Normandy, Rear Adml. Sir Philip Vian, commanding the Eastern Task Force, and Cdre. Douglas-Pennant, commanding the assault force for Gold Beach, also came on board, making *Apollo*'s bridge so crowded that Grindle sent his navigating officer to the wheelhouse below. This may have had some bearing on what was to follow.

"*Apollo* was steaming close inshore when she went the wrong side of a buoy and ran aground on a sand bar. Capt. Grindle boldly chose not to stop but to force the ship over.

"With much shuddering of the hull and whipping of the mast, he succeeded in this intention, at the cost of one propeller torn off and another shaft bent. *Apollo* disembarked her VIPs into another ship and went home at six knots.

"By an extraordinary coincidence the destroyer taking Gen. Montgomery on a similar tour of the beaches, also ran aground the next day, but Grindle was too generous a spirit to take any comfort from that.

"Gen. Eisenhower felt that he had in some way been responsible for what happened, and wrote a letter of mitigation to the First Sea Lord on Grindle's behalf. Grindle was none the less reprimanded by a court martial — after which one flag officer said to him, 'Join the club: we've all been reprimanded'."

We didn't go back to the beaches but were ordered to escort a force of carriers and battleships which was going to the Mediterranean and on through the Suez Canal to the Far Eastern Fleet.

We stopped for a few days in Algiers, and I particularly remember going ashore one evening, to the Casbah, where, in a night club, I witnessed amazing scenes which were quite shocking in my immature experience. We spent a few days in Alexandria, when our charges were safely through the Canal, and where we had our first experience of the amazing skill of the Egyptians in stealing everything. Despite an armed guard on the jetty, they managed to get away with some of the degaussing copperwire which surrounded our hull to give us protection against magnetic mines.

We were then sent to Malta to await a planned invasion of the south coast of France.

Whilst at Malta I managed to get a short leave and thumbed a lift in an RAF plane to Sicily in exchange for a bottle of gin to the pilot and stayed in a fantastic old monastery which had been converted into a hotel before the war, at Taormina, on a hill with a wonderful view including Mount Etna.

During the German occupation this had been the headquarters of General Kesselring and now it was in use as an officers' rest camp where one could stay for the equivalent of ten shillings a night. It was a beautiful place and now I believe is a very expensive hotel.

The ship itself then went to Sicily and we spent a short time in Catania, a beautiful big harbour. I remember that we were short of petrol for the ship's motorboat, but there were a number of Italian seaplanes and flying boats which had been sunk at their moorings in shallow water, and we were able to rob them of their fuel for the boat.

We also went to Taranto, another big natural harbour, and we were able to get some sailing in the boats of the local yacht club.

From there we went up to Bari, from where we were to give gun support to the Eighth Army which was slowly proceeding up the coast road but were continually held up by the German positions. We were able to bombard these positions with our main armament.

I can't remember how long these operations lasted, but eventually we were sent back to the U.K. to give the ship's company a short leave before we went east to join the British Pacific Fleet which was assembling at that time at Trincomalee in Ceylon.

Before we left England Lieut. Commander C.E.R. Sharp RN, took over the command of *Undaunted* from Lieut. Commander A. Mackenzie RNR.

With stops in Malta and Alexandria, we then went through the Suez Canal, which was a great excitement for me, and eventually found ourselves in the Red Sea, and so into the Indian Ocean where we were told to rendezvous with two troopships who were going to Bombay, and to escort them there.

On our way, and whilst we were near the Maldive Islands, we sighted an Arab dhow, and concern was felt that she might have a radio on board and would report the troopships to Japanese submarines. I was therefore sent in the ship's whaler with a small boarding party to check over the dhow.

I shall always remember, revolver in hand, climbing up the side of this lovely old dhow and being helped by the crew, and then searching the ship and finding no radio but being fascinated by how primitive she was in every way, unchanged for hundreds of years.

These dhows sailed backwards and forwards from Madagascar to India using the trade winds, and the only form of navigation that they had was a very old sextant, at least a hundred years old, and from its inscription made in Scotland, and probably stolen from a British ship. They did not know their position and we were able to give them this from our navigator, and they were also short of water. Cooking was done on a charcoal fire on deck.

The very ruffianly crew were obviously a bit intrigued by us, as we were by them, and having found nothing suspicious we returned to *Undaunted*, and eventually saw our troopships safely into Bombay.

We spent a few days there and were able to do a little sight-seeing, all of which was new and fascinating to me, and I remember the Towers of Silence in the Malabar Hills, where the dead are laid out on the top of the towers to be eaten by the vultures.

From Bombay we turned south, round the bottom of India, and up to Trincomalee on the east coast of Ceylon. Trincomalee is the tropical equivalent of Scapa Flow, a huge natural anchorage in which a large fleet can anchor and be totally safe. It had originally been colonised by the Dutch and some of their fortifications still stand.

Although like Scapa Flow there was nothing to do, we could swim and also sail the ship's whaler, and we were now in tropical rig of white shirts and shorts, and as the Fleet assembled it became quite social with lots of intership visits.

One of my father's partners in the City of London, and a lifelong friend of his, was Willie Gibb. I had always heard about his son James who had just started to work in the family business when he came down from Cambridge before the war, and it was always hoped by my father that I would do the same after the war. A letter from my father told me that James was in the aircraft carrier *Indomitable*, where he had been flying Seafires, the Fleet Air Arm equivalent of the Spitfire, and that *Indomitable* was due in Trincomalee as part of the Pacific Fleet.

One is always rather suspicious of children of one's parents' friends, as one is expected to like them, but which is not always the case. However, with James Gibb, whom I met for the first time there at Trincomalee, I liked him immediately. He was very personable, amusing and interesting, and after the war I was to join him in the business and we became firm friends until he died suddenly of a heart attack in 1979.

The British Pacific Fleet to be, which was assembling in Trincomalee, was to us an enormous and powerful fleet, but later, when we joined the American Task Force 57 in the Pacific, we realised that we were comparatively small.

We had 4 Fleet carriers, 4 battleships, 8 cruisers and 16

112

Undaunted in Pacific

destroyers, and the whole was supported by what was
known as the Fleet Train, which consisted of merchant
ships full of stores and ammunition, tankers, depot ships,
and so-called "Woolworth" aircraft carriers (which were
converted merchant ships) carrying spare aircraft for the
Fleet aircraft carriers. There must have been some 20,000
men manning this Fleet.

Eventually the Fleet received orders to proceed across
the Indian Ocean to Australia, but on the way to carry out
an attack on Sumatra in the Dutch East Indies, on a large
oil refinery which had been taken by the Japanese, at a
place called Palembang.

Planes from the carriers were to bomb the installation
and the battleships were to bombard with their big 14 inch
guns.

As the Fleet approached Palembang, we were attacked
by Japanese torpedo-carrying aircraft, which was a

fascinating sight. They suddenly appeared low above the horizon, flying towards us in line abreast, and there must have been nearly a dozen of them.

The whole Fleet opened fire with its guns, and one by one we saw these aircraft knocked down and crash into the sea. If they dropped any torpedoes they did not find a target, and the only casualties that we suffered were to one of the Fleet aircraft carriers, where a shell from one of our own ships had hit the "island" of the carrier and unfortunately caused some severe casualties.

Eventually we arrived at Fremantle, the port of Perth, on the west coast of Australia. This was the first time that the Australians had seen a British fleet, coming to support them against the Japanese, and they gave us a wonderful welcome which I described in a letter home as follows:

6 February 1945
". . . I now write to you from Australia. [This was Fremantle in Western Australia.] By the time we eventually stop somewhere, we shall have been at sea for a month, except for 12 hours in one port, getting in provisions.

A month at sea in a destroyer is a long time I can assure you, and I shall be very glad to get away from it in a few days. With any luck we shall get asked out to stay in peoples' houses for a few days.

However, we had a wonderful welcome when we first touched Australia.

We only had about 12 hours in, but in that time we were loaded down with food and fruit, and nobody could do enough for us. Every man in the fleet (some 20,000) received plum pudding, tinned fruit, sweets, chocolate, soap, writing paper, a pound of grapes, plums, apples and oranges — we were given books, and the ship swarmed with Red Cross representatives, people from the comforts fund, clergymen, and if only we could have had a few days in, we would have had a marvellous time. They are very hospitable in that part. I should also have liked an opportunity to have seen the country. Anyhow they seem to have an abundance of everything.

The chief change is in the weather, directly we left the tropics it got cold, and now I have to wear a sweater on the bridge, and sleep under a blanket at night. However I sleep much better, after all that heat. I hope it doesn't stay like it though, as I want to go surf bathing when we get in.

After all this time away from civilisation and a month at sea, we are going to thoroughly enjoy ourselves when we get the chance.

The sea has been rather rough for the last fortnight, and I am getting tired of banging about, because we always go everywhere so fast, and so the motion isn't too good . . ."

After a short rest we proceeded round the southern end of Australia and up the east coast to Sydney, where we had another wonderful welcome.

Sydney is a beautiful city, with a beautiful climate, built round a huge almost land-locked bay, which could accommodate several fleets like ours, and also had all the dockyard facilities that we would need. It was the main base in Australia of the combined American and British Pacific Fleet, Task Force 57 under the command of Admiral Chester Nimitz. The Americans also had naval bases in the islands to the north and across the Pacific.

Sydney was a wonderful place to be. There was every recreational facility and friendly faces, things which we had not seen for years in war-torn Britain. At this stage of the war the American Navy, Army and Air Force were gradually blasting and fighting their way across the Pacific, through the Japanese held islands, with the eventual objective of, if necessary, an armed landing in Japan, like Operation Overlord into Europe.

In joining the American Fleet we had to change several hallowed British naval practices, and learn an almost new language. Instead of a naval signal hoisted at the yardarm with flags, and then "close up" to the yardarm when the order was to be executed, we had to say that the signal was "two-blocked". Our motorboat became a "gasoline gig" and when our crew went ashore for short leave, the American ships piped the extraordinary (to us) call of "Liberty guys fall in".

The British ships were very popular with the American officers, because in our wardrooms we were allowed alcohol, and there was no alcohol in any American ship. We therefore had numerous US visitors.

The American Pacific Fleet must have been four or five times the size of our Fleet with a similar number in their Fleet Train, and the huge American manufacturing industry was turning out equipment, guns, planes, etc. by that time in enormous quantities so that there was, to us, an unimaginable wealth of equipment which contrasted with our experience of always being short of guns and equipment, and long delays in getting new advanced equipment as it was produced. For the first time we realised that we were the poor relations of the Americans.

After a period in Sydney the Fleet moved north up the east coast of Australia into the Tropics, and to the advanced base on the island of Manus. This was an Australian Protectorate and consisted of a huge anchorage which was really a shallow place in the ocean surrounded by coral reefs only a few feet high. A very large fleet could anchor here in safety.

We now started our combined operations with the American Fleet, mopping up the Japanese positions on the way to Tokyo and, hopefully, final victory.

Whenever the Fleet went to sea on operations we formed a giant circle with the 4 Fleet carriers in the middle together with the 4 battleships, outside them were the 8 cruisers, and on a four mile radius from the centre, also in a circle, were the 16 destroyers. We were therefore the outer protection for the cruisers and then the battleships and aircraft carriers.

The Fleet moved fast as a defence against submarine

attack and zigzagged, and when flying off aircraft or landing on aircraft, the whole Fleet would turn and steam into the wind, and all ships then turned together. Orders were given by the Admiral in command by radio with the loudspeaker on the bridge, except for zigzag course changes which followed a pattern which one knew and each leg meant an alteration of course at so many minutes past the hour.

The Officer of the Watch therefore had to be very much awake, especially at night, as a missed alteration of course might mean that you lost the Fleet or could be involved in a collision at speed with a capital ship which was not good for your destroyer. (In 1942, the cruiser HMS *Curacoa* was sliced in two by the Queen Mary which altered course in the dark and hit her.).

The Admiral's ship was the centre of the circle and you had to keep his ship on a constant bearing and at a constant distance. The distance was checked by radar, and there was a display on the bridge from which you could read off your distance and at night also the bearing. If, for one reason or another, the bearing began to change you had to increase or decrease your speed by instructing the engine room to either increase or decrease the revolutions of the propeller shafts. After a bit you became very adept at it, and it was really quite easy in daylight, but not so good at night, and even worse in bad weather at night.

When flying operations were in progress the Fleet increased speed to about 30 knots to give sufficient wind speed over the carriers' decks. Even so flying off a carrier, and especially flying on to a carrier, was a hazardous operation at the best of times, and if a plane had been damaged on operations it created further difficulties in getting it safely down.

The aircraft were controlled by the Fighter Direction Officer (FDO), and James Gibb was now one of the FDO's on *Indomitable*.

When landing, the aircraft lowered a hook which

hopefully engaged in a wire across the deck which ran out on hydraulic brakes and brought the aircraft to a halt in a very short distance. The aircraft would then be manhandled to the big deck lift and taken down into the hanger below the flight deck immediately. It was essential to keep the flight deck clear on operations, and if a plane was damaged on landing, or if before take off it had problems, the American practice was to retrieve the radio and a few other things from the aircraft, and then push it over the side to get it out of the way, because aircraft coming in were probably low on fuel and couldn't wait.

(HANGAR)

If aircraft crashed when coming back to the Fleet, which frequently happened, one of the destroyers' jobs was to pick up the pilot if he had survived.

When Task Force 57 was on operations against the Japanese, it could put some 2,500 aircraft into the air at a time for a strike, and there were also times when we closed a Japanese held island or later on the mainland of Japan, and the battleships bombarded the coast with their 14" guns from a distance of about 15 miles.

The Fleet would spend about two or three days on operations, during which time we would be in two watches, four hours on and four hours off, and at action stations when the shooting started.

After the two or three days of operations, the whole Fleet would retire about 500 miles to seaward, to meet the Fleet Train. This was an amazing sight as we closed them and the whole sea was full of seemingly hundreds of merchant ships, steaming in convoy formation.

As on these operations, we were at sea uninterruptedly for between two and three months at a time, the Fleet Train had to provide ammunition, oil fuel and food for all the ships. This was obtained by each ship knowing where it had to go and steaming alongside the supply ship, which maintained a steady course and speed. Supplies would be passed across on a taut wire on which travelled backwards and forwards a container with the stores. This was fairly

118

Lieut. M. Potter, DSC and the Author in the Pacific

easy in calm weather but very difficult in bad weather.

Oil fuel was obtained in a similar way by either steaming alongside a tanker, when an oil pipe would be passed across and connected to our ship and the oil fuel pumped across, or the tanker would trail a long hose from either quarter so that two ships could pick up the hoses, connect and get their oil fuel supply in that way.

New replacement aircraft were carried on the "Woolworth" carriers and we would pick up the pilots from the Fleet carrier and take them across to the "Woolworth" carrier, and they would then fly their aircraft back on to the Fleet carrier. This didn't always work because the "Woolworth" carriers were comparatively slow, doing at best about 18 or 20 knots. This was all right if there was enough wind, but in a calm it became very dicey.

In these circumstances we would follow along behind the

carrier, and if the plane did not get enough air speed to get off the deck, it would drop off the end of the flight deck of the carrier and into the sea, and we would then go and pick up the pilot, hopefully.

This happened quite often and it was amazing how many pilots we did pick up, including on one day two who shared the same cabin on the Fleet carrier.

After two or three days with the Fleet Train, the Fleet then returned to the operational area and began the whole process over again.

On these operations one lost any sense of the passing of time, other than being on or off watch, or at action stations, or eating and sleeping.

Food became very bad and we lived mostly on stews made from corned beef and tinned vegetables and hard (very hard) biscuits instead of bread.

When we were in the operational area, we were also subject to attack by the Japanese. Their fleet had been largely destroyed in earlier actions by the Americans, and we didn't seem to have too much trouble from their submarines, but attack by their aircraft was a constant worry.

In particular attacks by the Kamikaze pilots were very effective.

Kamikaze was a sacred wind which blew when Japan was in peril, and the pilots were trained with the belief that the highest duty that they could perform would be to die in battle for their homeland, and their method of attack was to commit suicide by diving their planes, laden with bombs, into an enemy ship.

Luckily they did not attack the destroyers on the outer screen, they were going for the carriers and the battleships in the centre, and it was an amazing sight to see one of these attacks. They dived almost vertically from a great height and it was very difficult for the ship's guns to destroy them before they themselves hit the ship and exploded. These attacks induced understandable terror in the gun crews.

The American carriers were particularly vulnerable because they had wooden flight decks, and the Kamikaze planes would go through these decks and explode in the hangers underneath, which would be full of aircraft with (HANGARS) full fuel tanks. Our own Fleet carriers had armoured decks and therefore the planes usually bounced off or exploded without penetrating into the hanger deck.

For us it was impossible to understand how anybody could commit suicide in this way and the Fleet was very frightened of this form of attack which was very effective.

However Task Force 57 survived and gradually pushed the Japanese back from the outer islands and eventually to the mainland of Japan.

The war was going well for the Allies and it now remained only for the final attack and landing in Japan which was expected to be achieved only with frightful losses to the Allied navies and armies, in view of the fanatical bravery of the Japanese soldiers and sailors.

By this time the war in Europe was over and we felt rather hard done by, still at war in the Pacific. However, the end came unexpectedly quickly. The Allies dropped atomic bombs on Hiroshima and Nagasaki, the Japanese capitulated, and finally the war was over in both Europe and the Pacific.

It was an amazing sense of relief because I think that we all knew subconsciously that the final onslaught was going to be very bloody, and that our chances of survival were fairly minimal.

Undoubtedly we had been saved by the atomic bomb, and whatever the moral argument may be against their use, I can only — from a personal and selfish point of view — thank heaven they dropped those bombs. After six years of war, it was very difficult to believe that at last the war was over, and we could consider our futures as civilians. As I had gone straight from school into the Navy I had never been a civilian.

My parents kept some of the letters that I wrote from the Pacific, and the following extracts give a good idea of life during those long periods at sea.

20 March 1945

". . . Where I am writing this from is just a shallow patch in the Pacific surrounded by coral reefs and with one or two bits of tree covered beach sticking up a few feet, in other words just a defended anchorage made by nature. There are an incredible number of ships here, and that is about all, there being no shore to put anything on.

You realise of course, that we are with the American Fleet now. The weather is still pretty hot, but there is a good breeze blowing. Bathing seems to be general in these places, although they are really quite open to the sea.

I haven't seen any sharks in any of these places, but we ran one down asleep on the water not very long ago — the wake was full of blood.

It is difficult to think of anything to write about these days, when we never get off the ship. On board all is much the same, we eat and sleep, go on watch, joke, quarrel, read, and that is just about all one can do.

I have read quite a lot recently including Nicholas Nickleby, A Time to Keep by Halliday Sutherland, and at the moment I am reading a very interesting book called The Long Weekend by Robert Graves and Michael Hodges.

Mail has to go about 15,000 miles to reach us, and I think the Airmail is very good . . ."

28 March 1945

". . . The weather is much cooler up here, so much so, in fact, that at night I have to wear a big sweater and battledress, and sleep under a blanket.

Still, I like it much better than the humid tropical heat. It is a nuisance always going from one type of climate to another, you can always get used to one but when you get cool and then go down into the tropics again, it is very uncomfortable. We move about such enormous distances, you have got to be prepared for any sort of weather.

The sea has been pretty rough, but is getting smoother now. All around the tropics you get tropical storms which are circular storms of varying size which move along definite paths. At their centre the wind is often about 100 m.p.h. and the weather is affected within about a one hundred mile radius.

They occur about once a month at this time of year, and are of course very important operationally, because they might wreck an amphibious operation completely. We have had quite a lot of time at action stations recently, but not many excitements.

The Americans certainly have got some equipment, they seem to have so many ships out here that I don't know how they use them.

Our own fleet seems comparatively small, they can put so many ships to sea for an operation.

What we don't like about these long operations is that in destroyers we can't carry very much food, and we are soon reduced to tins and dehydrated stuff which I hate. I read quite a lot of books which passes the time, but unfortunately we seem to be too far away for my wireless to pick up any music. The war seems to be going well in Europe, and it seems that we shall be able to smash the Germans this year. I think the Japanese war is going well. Japan will soon be completely cut off, and then invaded with an overwhelming superiority of equipment. All these thousands of Japs that are cut off will just be left to starve out and die, and I don't think they will last long in the hot, humid, and disease ridden tropical islands . . ."

5 *April 1945*
". . . Where we are now is warm again. A few months ago this place was top page news, and was possibly the turning point in the Pacific War, because the Japanese staked their Navy on it and lost. It is nice having the ship still for a bit, in bad weather you get so tired of the motion.

You fall over all the time, and every little thing you try to do, like shaving, is made ten times as difficult by

having to hang on, and you always lose your blance at
the wrong moment, and nothing will remain static . . ."

5 April 1945
". . . I had a letter from you and a letter from Anthony
on my birthday — a tanker brought it up. They take
about four weeks to get up here which isn't bad really.
They go to Sydney by air, then up to an advanced base by
air, and then out to the fleet in a supply ship or oiler. As
no doubt you have read in the papers, we are up in the
Ryukus. The weather is much cooler, but it has been
extremely rough for about a fortnight with very heavy
seas, which don't make for comfort. There must be a
typhoon about somewhere. According to the intelligence
the Ryukus aren't very nice. They are populated by about
100,000 inferior type Japanese and there are a great
number of wild boars, very poisonous snakes, great
numbers of rats and mosquitoes and almost every disease
under the sun, so I don't want to go ashore very much.
We have had a certain amount of resistance but nothing
serious, and everyone has shot down lots of planes. The
main trouble has been the food on board.

There is nothing fresh left, and our cooks are extremely
bad and unimaginative, meals are just an unpleasant
must.

We publish a newspaper every evening on board, the
W/T office tunes in to all the news throughout the day,
and then makes a summary.

I read a lot of books now, there is nothing else to do
when off watch. You get awfully tired of these long trips
of weeks and weeks at sea. I haven't been off the ship for
a month now except for an hour at an Officer's club once.
Macpherson is now engaged on Gibbons' Decline and Fall
of the R.E. If you would like to send me a book or two
they would be very welcome.

I expect you can see the strategy of this latest landing
out here. It now cuts Japan off completely from the world,
so she won't be able to reinforce Java and Sumatra etc.
except by land and that is very difficult. The American
Fleet is incredibly large and very good.

I think they will make some of our higher ups think twice about shaking up their ideas . . ."

6 April 1945

". . . It's stinking hot today, no wind and sun right overhead. Unfortunately there is no bathing as you can see the sharks swimming around, also lots of fish. It is an enormous anchorage here and rather lovely, high hills around the bay. I shall never believe there is a shortage of ships, there are thousands of them wherever we go. 99% American, we shall have to buck our ideas up after the war, if the Americans aren't going to run us off our feet in trade . . ."

13 April 1945

". . . The Australians are very proud to call themselves British, and especially so when they have been so swamped by Americans, of whom they are not very fond.

I am getting rather tired of continually being at sea, its so monotonous and we go to sea for about a month, then into some deserted non existent island where you top up and then out again.

I am longing to get off the ship and stretch my legs and get a change of scenery. The weather has been quite good recently, very little wind and a nice, not too hot, sun. Going into these American bases, one realises how extraordinarily bad our Navy is in providing relaxation and entertainment for officers and men. In all matters of equipment and facilities we are very much the poor relation of the American Fleet. Take Scapa, which has been a fleet base for some 30 years, anyway 5 years of this war. When we were there, there was one very mediocre cinema for the sailors and one or two very dingy church canteens, a flooded football ground, and quite a decent Officers Club. We've been into places that have only been cleared of Japs 2 or 3 months but in that time the Americans have achieved wonders. They get a beach, erect a small town round it, build enormous canteens, which provide food, iced beer, and ice cream in huge quantities for everyone, cinemas, theatres, shops, jeeps, in fact everything possible, and then they use landing craft and bring in 3 or 4000 men every afternoon. One place we went to, our sailors weren't allowed to go ashore to the U.S. place (anyway we had no boats or means of getting them there) but they were allowed to go to a deserted island in the harbour, where there was an aerodrome which they weren't allowed to go near, but for two hours they could go into a field and drink one bottle of beer supplied by the NAAFI and supervised by an officer. That is the usual sort of treatment that our sailors get and I think that it is all wrong. The Americans have every sort of comfort, etc. that is humanly possible to provide, and it is just the same with all Naval equipment, guns, etc. they get everything they want, and a lot of it is superior to ours.

Of course we have never fought this sort of war out here before, but it goes beyond that, we've always been so slow and conservative, and in the matter of welfare, the Navy has always been very bad.

Well, I must stop as the mail is closing, and a ship will come alongside and take the mail and put it on board another one that is going back to harbour, and then it will go in a plane to Sydney, and then by plane to England . . ."

30 April 1945

". . . I went ashore to the beach for a bathe the other day. It is quite a nice beach with black volcanic sand, and lots of palm trees. The only trouble is the sand, it must contain something which is a very good conductor, because it is so hot that you can't stand on it, and so getting into the water, you have to run like hell, but even then it burns! As you can imagine, close to the beach, the water is just like a hot bath, and so not very refreshing.

Our sailors have been quite contented while we are here, because they have been given 2½ pints of beer every day.

This is against all laws and traditions of the British

Navy, so somebody must have been very go ahead and brave.

It is a very good thing, because they can't go ashore, and with the beer, the cinema, bathing and sleeping in the sun they have been quite happy. I have organised several water polo games recently, and they are very popular. We have got quite a good team and we beat two aircraft carriers and the store ship we have been alongside. There is a terrific audience, and the opposing side get very brow beaten.

We are allowed to mention suicide bombing now. The Japanese have been using it now for a long time, and as you can imagine it is very effective and difficult to compete with, and of course we could never do the same thing ourselves. They have special suicide formations, known as Kamikaze attack units. Kamikaze is a mythical divine wind which blows away her enemies when Japan is in danger.

It must require an extraordinary mentality and outlook on life, to so willingly sacrifice yourself, something that we can't understand, but I suppose if you are brought up to believe something and nobody tries to give you any other ideas, it seems quite normal.

I have seen quite a few of these attacks and the whole thing is most astounding, a plane coming down in a screaming dive, and you may watch for about ten seconds knowing that it contains a man who is going to dash himself to death against a ship or go plunging into the sea, luckily most of the latter.

What on earth can you do with people who can do that sort of thing. I think we must exterminate Japan, and look on the Japanese as sub human beings, and if necessary, gas them out of all these islands, where they go on resisting until they are wiped out anyhow.

Perhaps by the time this letter reaches you, the war in Europe will be over. I do so hope for your sake that it will, and that all your worries will fade away. It must be such a relief that all the bombing is over, how people stood it for so long I don't know. As for me, I only want to get home, out of the Navy, settle down, and start my own life . . ."

8 May 1945

". . . Today you will be rejoicing in the end of the war in Europe, and what a relief it must be to you after all these painful years. I can still remember that first day, going down to the rubbish pit, mattress over the window, water in the baths, and the Maginot Line. Out here we can't help feeling rather sad, because we've still got a war here, and out here at sea it all seems rather remote and we don't feel like celebrating even if we could. I think I know how Cinderella felt when her sisters went off to the dance.

I don't think people in England think very much about the Pacific and even if they do they don't really understand what it is like.

A completely naval war, with its vast distances and consequent supply difficulties, months and months at sea at a time, heat and humidity, and an unnatural enemy.

Today the sky is completely overcast with very frequent rainstorms, the sea is rough with a lot of white horses, and so all the scuttles are shut to keep out the water, and that also keeps out the air, and so it is very hot below decks.

The sun may be obscured by clouds out here, but you can still feel it, and still get sunburnt. I expect you heard on the radio that we had been bombarding Sakashima, it is a pretty desolate looking place, but it is a staging point for planes coming from China and Formosa to Okinawa. The Japs are getting too fond of their suicide game . . ."

14 May 1945

". . . I listened to Churchill's speech on the end of the war, and I think he said something about it being a nice hot day. I was on watch at the time, and I had it relayed up to the bridge on one of the W/T loudspeakers. It was pouring with rain and I was soaked through and the visibility wasn't more than about 200 yards and I was trying to keep station in the fleet going about 20 knots, so I couldn't quite feel in the spirit of the occasion.

We had rather a nice New Zealand pilot, and one evening he was coming back to his carrier with a bit of engine trouble, and he was just going past us when someone rather light on the trigger opened fire (not us) and he crashed just ahead of us. When we got there, there was no plane, he was sitting quite happily in his dinghy, but I don't know how he got out, as the plane must have hit at about 200 knots.

We have had quite a lot of attacks lately, but luckily they always go for the big chaps . . .'

19 May 1945

". . . Time continues to pass unnoticed out here. I no longer think of days, you are either off or on watch up here, and after a bit you get into the swing of it, and you suddenly realise that so many weeks have gone. It is raining hard at the moment, and for the last few days it has been dead calm, and so rather stuffy. This morning I had to "witness" the opening of a barrel of rum (this happens about once a week). The rum store is right at the bottom of the ship aft, and there is no ventilation and it is always sealed up. The stench is indescribable, and after about 10 minutes you feel quite drunk! When the barrel is opened a measuring rod is put in and then it is topped up, so that an allowance is made for evaporation. As I expect you know, Navy rum is very strong and rough stuff, and I think in this climate it must be very bad for people. I never touch it, it's like petrol. I think a V2 rocket would go twice as far on it.

However, there would be an awful moan if you did try and stop it. The old sailors have got so used to it after about 20 years in the Navy that they couldn't do without it.

An issue of beer would be much better, but of course you couldn't carry enough, unless someone invented some beer powder.

We suffer very much from American news and radio out here, the BBC is coming through better now, and it is the only thing worth listening to. The American news never mentions anyone except themselves unless its bad news, when of course they make great play of it. Everything is wildly exaggerated and often untrue rumour, and I am heartily sick of Americans, American voices, and above all the "American way of life" as they like to call it. Not that they aren't efficient but I can't bear this awful "we are better than everyone else" complex. Unfortunately when the facts just aren't known, people really do believe in America that they won the war unaided. Our news is impartial, but I reckon the press in Germany was freer than the American radio and press. They still seem to hang on to the most extraordinary century old hates of us from the War of Independence. One thing that didn't go down well out here was a statement in the press, that the B.P.F. wasn't wanted out here and would be more nuisance than we were worth . . ."

29 May 1945
". . . During the last *two* months alone we have steamed 25,000 miles, if you work that out as a daily average you can see that this is quite a long way. Translate that into the fleet, and then into oil fuel for the fleet (we burn about 100 tons a day at that average speed) [and of course much more for a battleship or carrier] and then add food for some 20,000 men, bombs and shells and stores and spare parts and they come from England some 15,000 miles away and you begin to realise what sort of a supply problem it is.
And no ships have broken down in that time either.
When we get into harbour we are going to celebrate V.E. day in a big way, we shall have to make up for 3 months at sea and the prospect of a lot more . . ."

29 May 1945
". . . We are all very interested in the Government's plans for demobilisation, and if they release a group a fortnight as they are supposed to be doing I ought to get out in April '46.
However, everyone is a bit pessimistic about the Navy, it being so very much more of a skilled job than the others, you can't just train up anyone, and demobilisation

at that rate would just clean out the experienced and older key men.

Also being out here is a snag still I hope there won't be any delay.

Having a job to go to will be a great advantage. One thing I hope the Navy will do is to shorten the period of a foreign commission, 2–2½ years out here is an awful long time.

Take us for example, we have been at sea now for three months.

That means that the sailors have been living on top of each other, with no room to move, in messdecks whose ventilation is shocking, on tinned food, and in a very humid and hot climate, without any exercise or relaxation, and unable to get ashore, in fact nothing for them to do but go on and off watch, sleep, work, and eat. Two years at that pace is going to make its mark on people. Out here too you get a lot of skin diseases and the ship is alive with cockroaches (luckily no rats).

So I don't think people can complain if they do run wild when they *do* go ashore. They do too. Still, there's one thing, Sydney has made a great impression on them all, and they are all well fixed up ashore, everyone seems to have got some family who has semi-adopted them, and of course they have plenty of money after being at sea for some time. The last few days the sea has been dead calm with a lot of cumulus cloud and lovely sunsets, and at night a full moon, and you can stay up all night without a shirt. I enclose a few photos taken of us coming alongside a battleship for meat and bread. Note that we are very dirty, no pretty paintwork out here. Everything from people to mail goes from ship to ship in a bag on a rope, and it hasn't broken yet.

When we are in the fuelling area quite a traffic goes on, destroyers go round all the ships, people go from one ship to another, pilots go to ferrying carriers to pick up new aircraft, inter ship mail has to be delivered, in fact the big ships are like large houses and we get employed delivering the groceries etc . . ."

3 June 1945

". . . I am so glad to hear you have got a petrol ration again, I know how much that means to you.

Well, the climate is much better the further we get South (the sun is north of the equator now), it is not so humid now, and when the sun has gone there is quite a nip in the air, butter and chocolate are solids again, cold water comes out of the cold tap, and you have to sleep under a sheet at night. We had one night at an advanced anchorage the other day, and I got a lot of mail.

We celebrated V.E. day by drinking all our champagne and quite a lot else, and nobody felt very bright the next day. I had James Gibb over for dinner, he is very well but rather tired from overwork. In the operational area he is closed up in the Aircraft Directing Room from 4.30 AM till 8.00 at night, and no breaks except for occasional sandwiches. A few months of that takes it out of you, also carriers aren't exactly safe to be in because all the bombs go straight for them. He gets rather bored with the ship in harbour too because the large number of very youthful Fleet Air Arm pilots are invariably violently drunk, and in the wardroom, though the pilots are not flying, most of the furniture, and quite a lot of bottles, are. This is a F.A.A. prerogative, and when you take into account their job, they are entitled to it. So he was quite glad to come across.

Well, I hope you are all rapidly getting back to normal, that's what I want to see when I come back, everything back to normal and as it was in 1939 at home.

The weather has been fairly rough for the last two days and as we have been going rather fast, it has been rather uncomfortable.

Since we left England we have steamed 56,000 miles, not bad going when you come to think of it. When I leave the Navy I shall have covered quite a long way and seen quite a few countries . . ."

17 June 1945

". . . I came back this morning from my four days leave which went all too quickly. We went away to the Blue

132

Mountains in Bill's car (it is about 90 miles). We went to a hotel at a small village called Kurrajong. It is in the foothills and about 1500 ft up. Unfortunately the weather has been terrible lately, terrific storms and torrential rains. Normally it would have been lovely up there, with a wonderful view over the plain, and very pretty country amongst the orange and lemon groves.

We stayed for two days, but you couldn't go out, and it became rather boring so we decided to go back to Bill's home. We couldn't go back by the way we came, because the bridge over the Hawkesbury river was by then 5 ft under water, and so we had to go back over the mountains.

The floods have been very extensive and whole towns inundated.

We had to cross a 4000 ft spur and it was quite cold, but after driving about 130 miles we got through and back home.

Yesterday we went for a picnic in the yacht, and cooked chops and sausages at four in the afternoon. In the evening we went to Princes, which is the best night club where you have dinner and dancing, it compares favourably with anything in London. I had rather too much champagne (some of it Moet '28) and I enjoyed myself.

Mealtimes in this country are odd, you don't have afternoon tea, but dinner at 6.30 and then an equally large supper at 1000.

Breakfast of steak and eggs is nothing unusual — this is a country of big eats! Suits me. The weather has really been foul though, rain and rain.

I saw that horror film about the concentration camps the other day — it really is frightful, we can *never* forgive them for that, and that film ought to be shown to everyone every ten years or so, otherwise we shall forget and forgive . . ."

18 July 1945
". . . The weather is playing all sorts of tricks up here. The other day, it was extremely cold and I was wearing

my flying boots and two sweaters on watch, but the last day it has been moderately warm, pouring with rain, and this afternoon thick sea mist, with the direction of the swell and wind 90° different — I think there is a typhoon about fairly close. I expect you hear on the wireless what we are doing, the Americans certainly believe in hitting the headlines.

Now that we have absolute seapower even on Japan's front door, the war will progress faster. We and the Americans have a tremendous concentration of ships up here.

All the beards are going well, and everyone is looking pretty scruffy. Mine is no longer uncomfortable, and it is quite a good thing if the weather is cold, or if you sleep late in the mornings.

On the food line we are down to corned beef and dehydrated potatoes.

To add to the crowd in the wardroom we have now got a pilot with us.

He was hit by flak over Tokyo, and was going to bale out over the fleet but couldn't get his cockpit cover open, and while he was wrestling with it, he didn't look where he was going, and flew into the sea. How he survived I can't imagine, he just woke up swimmimg, and apart from a few bruises and cuts he is quite alright. He is a very nice type.

We ought to get some mail in a few days. I haven't had one from you for a fortnight.

Passing through the tropics I got very sunburnt, and now I am peeling all over which is rather a nuisance.

I like that book of English Essays you sent me, there are some very amusing ones in it . . . .''

19th.

The weather is bad today, a big swell and we are rolling like a pig as we are rather light on fuel. It's very difficult to think of anything to write about on operations like this, as you can never mention anything. I see the press reports mentioned the *Undine* and *Grenville*, both of our flotilla, so if you ever hear of them, or any other U's, remember that we are with them, and we have done all the hard work so far but have not been mentioned.

Our wireless and gramophone have broken which is a bore as we don't get any news now, and we shan't be able to get them working again for a long time.

When we next go back to civilisation we are about due for a short refit, and ought to get a few weeks leave. I thought of going skiing, or perhaps flying somewhere different like Tasmania . . ."

25 July 1945

". . . The weather has been pretty hot again lately, but there has been a lot of wind, and the sea has been rough for a while now.

We picked up another pilot the other day, who not only came from the same carrier as the last one, but shared a cabin with him! Quite a coincidence.

He was quite unhurt and gave us all his equipment, they get issued with very good stuff. It's typical of the Navy, that if you lose an aircraft, no-one bothers to give it another thought, but if you had 10/- of your own in your wallet and lost it when you were in the water, you would have to fill in about fifty forms and move Heaven and earth, before you got it refunded.

My beard is three weeks old now, and I'm told I look like a beach comber — I feel rather dirty. Still I shall keep it until we go back to civilisation and then off it comes for good. It's just one of those things you have to do once in your life, but you don't get much opportunity in the office.

We've been at sea four weeks now, and it has gone quite quickly. Once you have resigned yourself to not seeing land for a few months, and got into a routine of eating, sleeping and reading, and developed a state of mind where you never think of the future, but live entirely in the present, then you suddenly find the time has flown and you are back in harbour again. The milestones are of course the days when the mail comes up. You have several duty destroyers who go round all the ships collecting and delivering, and it is quite amusing as you get on board all sorts of odd things from passengers and war correspondents to eggs and aeroplane propellers. On "Strike" days when we are operating, we spend the whole time going to action stations which gets rather boring, normally we are four hours on and four off, but there are so many planes about that it is very easy to get mixed up, and whenever a plane is unidentified we go to action stations. The suicide boys or Kamikaze kids haven't been so active this time though luckily.

We had a supply ship up the other day and managed to get some potatoes, apples and cheese, which has improved the diet for a few days. In the operating area though, the whole ship goes on "Pot Mess", which is a gigantic stew for everybody, with everything possible in it . . ."

30 July 1945

". . . Life continues in the same groove here, and will remain so for a few weeks. The weather continues very uncertain with a lot of wind and swell. It changes so very quickly, one moment it is a lovely day and very hot, and a few hours later a cold damp sea mist has closed in, which isn't good for flying.

I had a fine view of a rather spectacular Jap swatting the other day. A Jap torpedo bomber was shot down from about 25,000 ft above the fleet, and he came down in a power dive faster and faster until the wings and tailplane came off and the crew baled out. The fuselage came on at about 700 m.p.h. with the engine revving all out and making an agonised screaming noise.

The pilot arrived dead about 15 mins later by parachute while the other bits floated down like leaves, burning. It was like a Hollywood film, coming down in a vertical dive and then the wings breaking off.

It is very depressing to hear about the Labour party, England will be a difficult country to live in for a few years yet. I can't imagine Bevin as foreign secretary. Having seen what a Labour government has done to Australia, I feel even more depressed. There, the government is despised by all and has no authority because nobody takes much notice of it, and all the trade unions say "Boo" to it, and it doesn't say "Boo" back. It is the same with food and petrol rationing and with licensing laws, they are just openly disregarded completely. The result is that everyone strikes when they want a holiday, and they always get their own way.

I had to stop writing for ten minutes and go to action stations — a very frequent occurrence these days — one twin engined recce plane came over and was shot down.

Well, my love to everyone, and let's hope this war is soon over. Your letters and papers are very welcome, and make all the difference to these long months at sea, so far away from home . . ."

5 August 1945

". . . We have been having quite good weather lately, clear days but a very big swell, which means that another typhoon is about, but we keep clear of them. They are getting more frequent at this time of year, and they can be extremely dangerous, as the Americans have found to their cost on several occasions.

I am getting tired of seeing nothing but the sea, and also getting no exercise — you get very constipated as a result of that, also thru' lack of any fresh food — and shall be glad one of these days to see some civilisation again. We left the latter at the end of June, and have seen nothing but other ships since. At the moment we have "camping" in the wardroom two BBC representatives. One of them is a Canadian by name Stanley Maxted. He is extremly nice, and a very able commentator.

He landed at Arnhem by parachute, and had a pretty tough time, and at the crossing of the Rhine he went by glider, but was shot down behind the German lines. He was wounded and injured in the crash but did his job. He is a very quiet man and 48 years old, an age at which I shouldn't want to start parachuting. He did a very good broadcast on his experiences to the ship's company.

They have got the most ingenious recording machine, and it will be just the thing for the office, as it is simple and cheap. Your voice is turned into electric impulses

137

which are fed into an electromagnet. Running through the magnet from one reel to another is a thin steel wire, which as it runs thru' is magnetised by the electromagnet to a greater or less extent by the impulses generated by your voice. When you have finished all you have to do is to run it through again, and the magnetised wire sets up impulses in the magnet which come out as speech. So instead of having a typist at home, you merely dictate your letters into the machine and then take your reel of wire up to the office where the typist can play it and type it . . ."

8 August 1945

". . . Another nice batch of letters arrived from you the other day. First of all I am disappointed you don't like my photo, and always say I look thin, or as Rosemary says, pathetic! I always have been thin, I sweat a lot but I don't get any exercise, so that ought to make all things equal. Anyway I can assure you that I am very well, although too long in this climate and under these conditions doesn't help.

Demobilisation seems to be going along well, and we expect to lose up to age group 25 at the end of next month.

Unfortunately, officers are not going so fast. I can assure you that I am doing nothing to retard my exit.

It is going to be difficult after six years of a life like this to change one's habits and daily life. I think I shall find it very odd to begin with. I shan't know what to do with myself at first, I don't know anyone at home and I shall have to find and start fresh interests all over again. It will be difficult starting in the office too, I shall feel awkward because I shan't know anything, and will probably have to learn it in competition with people much younger than myself. I hope you will understand. I hope England won't be too broken after the war and that everyone won't be too poor.

I think I should like to take up gliding, its the best form of flying and requires more skill, also its cheaper. It's rather fun on long night watches thinking of these

138

things, and I only hope some of them will materialise. It's very hot today, and it's too hot to go down into my cabin, and I could do with a good bathe.

I am reading a very interesting book called "Maquis" at the moment. The weather has been lovely and calm lately, but that is not usual for this is the season of typhoons. My acquaintance with the Pacific so far by no means bears out the name . . ."

14 August 1945
". . . The news seems wonderful, and I think the war will be over in a few more days. It was three in the morning when we picked up the news and I was on watch.

The whole ship immediately woke up and all the sailors got a "tot" of rum out from somewhere and started celebrating. The weather is getting cooler now, and we shall be in blues again in a couple of days. I am looking forward to a good whack of leave, about 14 days I hope.

A lot of letters have been arriving burnt — there was an air crash at Sydney.

Until today, the weather has been lovely although extremely hot. Soft colouring and lovely sunsets, also the sea has been very calm. Some of the islands really look as you imagine they ought to. John Meares is on his way up here, and I am hoping we may cross in harbour and not at sea, otherwise I shan't have a chance of seeing him for a bit. I haven't seen James Gibb for a couple of months, they have been refitting. I am looking forward to a surfeit of oysters and chicken in a few days time, they taste even better after you have been living out of tins for a bit. There was quite a riot in Sydney the other day, I believe. Somebody broadcasted that the war was over, and everyone had a party, set fire to houses, and overturned fire engines. Perhaps by the time I write next the war *will* be over, we shall certainly have earned a peace . . ."

16 August 1945
". . . Well, at last the wonderful day has come, and it seems too incredible to believe — six years is a long time.

As I stood in the Wireless Office listening to Attlee surrounded by as many of the ship's company as could squeeze in, my mind went back to Sept 3rd 1939 when Chamberlain announced that a state of war existed, how little did we guess or could we comprehend what lay ahead, until yesterday when it all came to an end. If we had thought or realised in 1939 that six weary years of horrors lay ahead, I don't think we could have faced it. There will be a lot to do out here for a few months but it won't be long now before I come home and start being a civilian again. I am proud that I served through the whole war, and that during that whole time I took an active part in the fighting, and I think that that was the least that could be expected of those of us who had a better start in life than most others. I think the war has shown that this generation wasn't decadent after all.

I can imagine how thankful you must be feeling, now that it is all ending. We were young and adaptable, and the war wasn't perhaps such a catastrophe, but for your generation, to have to endure a second war, and to see your world that you had built and believed in, falling to bits about you, and your children and belongings taken away from you, it must have been very hard.

Everyone on board celebrated V.J. day. It meant far more to us out here than V.E. day, but I expect the opposite was true with you. We were doing some gunnery practice at the time, and we were passing fairly close to a merchant ship who must have thought we were celebrating and firing for fun, because she suddenly started firing all her guns in the air, together with rockets, etc. and having a high old time. They obviously thought they weren't going to be out done by any of H.M. Ships.

Well, tomorrow we shall go ashore for the first time for two months and more, and it certainly will feel good. My love to everyone and let's hope we shall all be together again very soon . . ."

* * *

From a Sydney Newspaper
"Warship comes in flying Enemy Flags."

Ferry passengers on the Harbor this morning could hardly believe their eyes when they saw a rusty, battle-stained warship bearing down on them flying both the Japanese ensign and Nazi Swastika.

The vessel was the destroyer HMS *Undaunted*, first British warship to arrive in Sydney since peace was declared.

At her masthead she had the "BUS" flag (a V-flag flown by British and American vessels engaged on combined operations) and under it the British, American, French, Greek, Polish, Chinese, Japanese, and German ensigns.

"We were feeling rather exuberant, so we hoisted the whole bang lot as we came through the Heads," said one of the *Undaunted*'s officers.

The *Undaunted* was in the Coral Sea when the peace message came through, and "spliced the mainbrace" in true Navy tradition.

The men, however, are looking forward to having their real celebrations in port, for they were at sea off Sakashima when the VE-Day announcement also was made.

Since leaving Sydney in June, the *Undaunted* has been operating under American control with the Third Fleet.

Most hectic experience of this patrol was when a diving suicide plane was shot down by a Seafire right above her decks.

She was to have taken part in one of the huge naval bombardments of Japan, but this was cancelled when typhoon reports were received.

One of her most prized possessions is General Dwight Eisenhower's personal flag, bearing his signature on one of the white stars, which he gave to the ship's company when on board.

Today her complement was busy scraping the paint off the brass fittings to prepare the ship for peace-time dress."

Historical Note
There were earlier ships called *Undaunted* in the Royal Navy, and in May 1814 HMS *Undaunted* carried the defeated Emperor Napoleon Bonaparte to exile on the island of Elba.

One hundred and thirty years later, HMS *Undaunted* carried the about to be victorious Allied Commanders back from the Normandy beaches to England.

CHAPTER 7

PEACE AT LAST

When the Fleet had returned to Sydney, we were sent down to Devonport Dockyard, at Auckland in New Zealand, for a much needed refit, which, but for the end of the war, would have been to prepare us for the final attack on the Japanese Mainland.

This was a very pleasant interlude and I spent two weeks' leave with Michael Potter at a sheep station in North Island. This was an idyllic place to have a complete rest and the farm that we stayed on was what I imagined Victorian country life to have been like in England.

There were two big adjacent farms owned by two brothers who had both married sisters from Scotland. They were completely self-supporting from their own food, the children went to school on their ponies, and the country was green and beautiful, and our hosts were very hospitable. I described this in letters home as follows:—

13 September 1945
". . . I am now staying on a farm in what is known as the Waikato district.

The country is very lovely, rolling open hills and very green paddocks, and nothing in sight except sheep and cows.

The house is set on a slight hill and is built of sandstone, like Charterhouse Chapel, which is very unusual out here.

They have a nice garden surrounding the house and the view out over the hills is lovely. Mr George Vosper is a typical sheep farmer, very tough and burly and walks

about in incredible old clothes. Mrs comes from
Edinburgh and is very nice and homely. The next farm
about 5 miles away is owned by his brother who married
Mrs' sister. The nearest town Cambridge is about nine miles away
and is just a broad main street with trees down each side
and lined with the few shops — in fact it is just like a
wild west town except that there is no hitching post for
the horses outside the local saloon.

15th. All the neighbouring farms are owned by brothers
and cousins, and they all have very nice houses. It is very
much a land of plenty round here, I have all the milk and
cream I can eat and more, turkeys are wild round here
and you just shoot one when you want one.

At the moment we have been living on lamb and
turkey. Everyone has lots of lovely horses and they use
them as we use bicycles — children go to school on them,
and of course it is the only way to get about the farm.
The houses are all modern and comfortable with electric
cooking and refrigerators.

Farming is of course very hard work but they all seem
fairly comfortably off.

There is a daughter who is a very nice girl and very
capable, she rides beautifully and rounds up the sheep for
papa. I rode her horse the other day and couldn't hold it
and set off wildly at full gallop and couldn't stop it.

After about a mile across the paddock it stopped very
suddenly and I went on, my foot caught in the stirrup but
luckily the strap broke. I was carrying a milkcan which
may have frightened it, and my fall broke the milkcan.

The same thing happened on the way back except that I
stayed on this time.

The weather has been quite nice, although some days it
has drizzled. There are ten motherless lambs on the front
lawn and I have to feed them three times a day out of a
bottle. They are very sweet things and it is a pity they
grow up into such silly ugly things. We have driven quite
a lot around the surrounding country and visited all the
relations. Nearly all the people out here either came out
here in their youth or their parents did, and they always

want to talk about the "Old Country". This morning we have been very busy "docking lambs". You ride out over the hills and round up the sheep with dogs and drive them into a pen, and then the fun begins trying to catch the lambs. They all go rushing round with their Mothers and you have to seize them and carry them to Jim the Maori who holds them while Mr Vosper does the necessary.

As you can imagine you get quite dirty, and we did 200 lambs before lunch. On a really good day they do about 800.

This is the best riding country I have ever seen, the trees are only in odd clumps, otherwise the hills roll smoothly away with nothing but green grass and the occasional fence. If you don't ride about the farm, you go on a sledge drawn by two big carthorses and it is just as good riding over the grass as if you were on snow. We wanted some lamb for the house the other day, so I watched Mr Vosper catch a lamb (at least a sheep about a year old), shear it, kill it, skin it, clean it and hanging up in the larder in joints all in about ¾ hour.

This place is called Maungatantari, as is also the mountain which we are at the foot of, the Maori names are very pretty although rather a mouthful, the next brother's farm is called Whareola which means "house of health". Yesterday we went to a place called Morrinsville about 28 miles away, where there was a big cattle sale, and Pa wanted to browse around and the daughter had bought a polo pony, which she then proceeded to ride home — quite a long way for a girl by herself. The nearest railway is over 20 miles away, so up here there isn't a sound to be heard except for the cattle and the wind and the birds. Most evenings the various families congregate in somebody's house and we play crocquet and billiards etc. It must be a lonely life at times, but that must be compensated for by living in such nice surroundings. It is very like some parts of Scotland (like Golspie) but of course much warmer in the summer and I should think things grow better here. Lemons and oranges grow in the garden. New Zealand is just one big farmers country and the towns are just centres where the produce is collected and the farmers come in once a week to shop, not unlike Reading but not nearly as solidly built. Nearly all houses are of wood out here, and are always one storey. I think England must have been like this 100 years ago, without the modern conveniences.

They have a telephone here but there are also about five other people on the same line, and you have a special call, so of course everybody listens to everyone else. We hope to drive to Rotarua next week, Pa is very keen to show us it, and I want to go very much. This is a wonderful change as you can imagine and I am enjoying every minute, and to be out in the open country, right away from everybody, on a horse and with sheep dogs is just marvellous.

I wish you could be here too and enjoy all the milk, cream, eggs and fresh meat. You have to be very careful to agree with everything Mr Vosper says, as he is very blunt and says just what he thinks. He wanted us to go to the local football match, but luckily he has decided to get some ploughing done, and I am having a pleasantly quiet afternoon. Mrs' third sister came to dinner last night, she married a farmer next door the other way.

Grandpapa lives in this house, so they really are quite a family. They talk about Scotland all the time, which annoys Mr Vosper. Grandpa is 85 but very sprightly . . ."

23 September 1945

". . . I forgot to tell you in my last letter of our trip to Rotarua, the hot springs' district. We drove over from Cambridge which is about 60 miles way. The drive was very lovely, over a range of hills called the Mamacoos and through very densely overgrown forest which are called native bush, there are all sorts of flowering trees and creepers and a lot of tree ferns. There were very fine views from the hills. The town of Rotarua is a nondescript untidy looking place on the shores of Lake Rotarua, which is a fine big fresh water lake surrounded by mountains.

The whole place stinks of hydrogen sulphide as if someone had done an oversized fart, and I should hate to live there. The atmosphere is so sulphury that silver turns black very quickly. It's a queer place, these hot springs bob up all over the place, and you see steam rising out of the earth in gardens and fields and ditches, and it looks rather like a town the morning after the blitz. The most active part is up a valley and is enclosed as a reserve. In here you can feel the earth rumbling and they have frequent earthquakes.

Every few yards there is a hole in the ground from which comes steam or boiling water and all the rocks are covered with yellow sulphur and a white deposit. There are big holes and small holes, cracks in the ground and geysers, pools of boiling mud — in fact you can imagine it as a very fine Old Testament Hell. The geysers only play occasionally with any force, but we were lucky and were sitting looking at one when it went off and threw a column of water and steam about 100 feet into the air with much noise — very impressive. Boiling mud pools are rather fascinating, they are rather like a big saucepan of porridge on the boil, big bubbles going "blip-blurp". I thought it would be a fine place for a murder. You have to be very careful as at any moment the ground might cave in under you or a jet of boiling water shoot out of a hole, and all the time the earth rumbled and hissed and was very warm to the feet.

It was all very interesting and certainly worth seeing. There are also lovely springs of water and pools which are thick with rainbow trout . . ."

12 October 1945

". . . We have been slightly delayed I am glad to say, but expect to go about next Thursday. I have had a cold the last few days which has been rather annoying, and have stayed aboard.

This week we have had a round of cocktail parties which have been rather a bore. First there was one for foremen and chargehands of the yard, they just swallow beer in large quantities. Next we had the yacht squadron, this consists of a lot of old boffins who think they are awful dogs, they are very hearty and tell dirty stories all the time. We gave them our new cocktail "Atomic bomb" which polished them off, and they were all reeling about the place when they left. Next night it was the Commodore and all the local officers and wives, and it was much better than the others. Last Saturday I had a lovely ride, I had a really good horse and we had some very good exercise, too good really, as the woman didn't look very pleased when we brought the horses back rather warm.

We went to a film and then dancing in the evening. I have had a car lately, which makes all the difference. I share it with the Engineer Officer. We have two other cars to the wardroom's name, so we aren't too badly off. Sunday afternoon we went up to a friend's house and played cards during the afternoon and then went for a walk along the beach. The coasts around Auckland are very lovely — the whole is a maze of islands and a yachtsman's paradise, you can sail for days without getting out of sheltered waters. The extinct volcano, Rangitoto, which dominates the harbour is very beautiful.

We picked oysters off the rocks and ate them.

Tomorrow, we are driving out (four of us) to have a picnic, then we shall go somewhere in the evening to dance. A lot of ex Jap P.O.W.'s are arriving here to recover in the temperate climate. We had one on board for lunch the other day. He was a Fleet Air Arm pilot shot down in the Indian Ocean from the *Illustrious* a year ago. He looked very ill and when rescued had been paralysed in legs and arms. You could see his nerves were very bad, as his hands shook all the time. He had been in a secret camp near Tokyo where they kept flying and submarine officers in solitary confinement and tortured them to get information.

He had been interrogated on and off for a year by an ex Cambridge undergraduate!! That's gratitude. He had been reported killed to his parents, so they must have been very elated to hear the news . . ."

148

CHAPTER 8

FINAL DAYS

After *Undaunted*'s refit was completed, she was ordered to proceed to Hong Kong via Sydney, and it was on the voyage to Sydney that I became very ill with a high temperature and fever, so that when we arrived in Sydney I was immediately put ashore and into a local hospital, as nobody knew what my problem was. They thought it was pneumonia, but eventually decided that I had glandular fever and jaundice together.

I was certainly very ill and in a hospital which was full of Australian and British troops who had been prisoners of war in Japanese hands, having been taken prisoner in Singapore, who were in a much worse state than I was, suffering from beri-beri and general malnutrition.

Many years later when I was living in Hampshire and employed a local man as a part-time gardener, I discovered one day, that he had been one of these prisoners of war and had been in this same hospital at about the same time. I learned from him and from others about the terrible treatment that prisoners received from the Japanese.

When I recovered and was discharged from hospital, *Undaunted* had gone to Hong Kong and nobody particularly wanted to own me, and so in order to convalesce, I accepted the kind offer of an Australian family who lived in Queensland, and who farmed inland from Brisbane who asked me to come up and stay on their cattle station.

I managed to get a flight from Sydney up to Brisbane where they met me and took me by car to their home.

Like the family in New Zealand, they were incredibly hospitable and nice, and with plenty of good food and rest I soon recovered and was able to take part, with the family, in the operations of their cattle ranch.

It was beautiful country, they had a mob of horses in a paddock in front of the house, and you rode any horse that you could catch. I wrote a long letter home about this visit.

27 November 1945

". . . I arrived back, by plane, in Sydney this afternoon, and am back at the hospital. I feel very well after my leave, and am very sunburnt. I was a bit late getting back, as I couldn't get on the plane the day I intended (yesterday), and it started very late this morning. I came down in a Dakota, which was rather uncomfortable, but it wasn't so bumpy as on the way up.

It is much cooler down here than in Brisbane, but I liked what I saw of Brisbane. I spent two nights there staying at the biggest hotel which is run by the Queensland Temperance League — you have to sign a chit to say that you won't drink in your room!

I very much enjoyed my 14 days with the Mackenzies, she was particularly nice, and very hard working and capable. She has to do everything herself — cooking, cleaning, laundering and she doesn't have any neighbours to chat with within five miles.

One thing I particularly enjoyed was mustering cattle, and driving them about. It was very strenuous work. Cattle pick up bloodsucking ticks, and so they have to be dipped every so often, and you do an area each day, until they are all done.

We used to start out about 7.30 and it would probably take an hour to ride to the top of the country you were going to muster. You ride down all the gullies, creeks, and valleys and round up all the cattle and keep them in a mob and take them down to the dip. They are very wild and try and break away most of the time, and you have to ride after them at full gallop and head them off and bring them back.

The Australians ride differently to us and I prefer their

way now. The saddle is much more of a seat and so not so tiring, and it has sort of built up bits in front of your knees which keeps them in place. You ride with the stirrups very long, so that the leg is only just bent, and you stand up in the stirrups, leaning right forward holding the reins very short and with your hands either side of the horse's head, almost below his ears. You can then go galloping down gulleys, full of holes and trees, round rocks etc. after the cattle, without any difficulty at all and have complete control of the horse. The country there is very hilly, with broad open valleys, but the hills are very thickly covered with gum trees. In order to make the grass grow for the cattle to eat, the trees have to be thinned. They do this by "ringbarking" about every other one. They cut the bark off round the trunk for a small part of it, and after 12 months the tree dies.

But they remain standing for some time, and this gives all the country a rather petrified unsatisfactory look, with these dead trees everywhere. Lots of them, of course, are down, and you spend all your time jumping over them, which makes it all the more exciting riding.

Riding through the woods, wallabies go jumping away, looking rather like greyhounds in the distance. Parrots fly about in the trees. At lunch time you stop on the banks of a stream, make a fire, fill up the billy from the stream and make the tea. The ants are rather a nuisance though, much bigger than our kind, about ¼ inch long and some of them bite. Everywhere you look are anthills about 5−6 feet high. The cattlemen paid me a great compliment apparently, when 2 of them told Mr Mackenzie that the way I rode after the cattle, I should soon make a good cattleman with a little experience. I learnt to crack a stock whip too, though I seemed to hit myself rather frequently.

There was an old gardener who was a great character. He was 73 and lived in a cottage adjoining the house, and worked in the garden about 10 hours daily and took a great pride in everything.

He refused to draw his pension or any wages from Mr Mackenzie, as he said he was quite happy without it. He had all his meals in the kitchen, and occasionally went to Brisbane for the weekend to go to the races, which was one of his main interests, he was tall and upright, with a rather striking face. Any Australian living in the country is extremely independent like that, and everyone, whether they are cattlemen, farm labourers, etc. or station owners/managers treat each other as equals, so that when Alf, the gardener, wanted to go to the races, Papa got up at 6.00 in the morning to drive him in to the station, and he was met again the following evening. You can understand it of course when everyone shares a hard life, and works together.

I found riding about 10 hours a day very sore making for the old behind at first, and we went mustering for four days running, me in a pair of breeches which were much too small and which split when I bent over too far, and a "diggers" hat which is extremely necessary, as the sun is very, very hot. In summer it gets so hot that it kills *all* the plants in the garden, and you have to plant *all* your flowers every spring. I am sending you an envelope with some passion fruit seeds in it. Just plant them in the spring in a warm spot and let them grow over some wire or something just as they like. They grow in Melbourne, whose climate is very similar to south England. I ate enormous quantities of them, with sugar and cream. Strawberries up there bear fruit for about six months, and I also gorged myself on them. The telephone up there amused me, it only works from 0900 to 1600 daily except for weekends when it doesn't work at all after Saturday midday.

I think I put on lots of weight but lost it all riding! . . ."

However, all good things had to come to an end, and eventually I went back to Sydney, drew my pay, and began to think how I was going to get back to England.

I applied to the local naval authorities for a passage, and eventually I was told that I could join the frigate *Enchantress*, which also served as the First Lord of the Admiralty's yacht, when he needed one, and had been

152

used by Mr Duff Cooper and also by Mr A.V. Alexander. She was due to leave Sydney for the UK at the end of December 1945, travelling without any other ships, and I moved on board to a very comfortable cabin and made friends with the Ship's Doctor.

It was decided by the Captain, and supported by the other officers, that we didn't want to get back to England until the spring and therefore we should enjoy our voyage and stop at as many places as possible on the way, so that we didn't get to England until April at the earliest. We finally left Melbourne on New Year's Day 1946.

As far as I can remember we stopped in Fremantle, then across to India, to Aden, to Port Said, Suez, Alexandria, Malta, Gibraltar and finally to Portsmouth.

It seemed rather an anticlimax to be back in England again, the war over, and our thoughts on demobilisation.

My father drove down to Portsmouth to meet me and that was the last time I saw any of HM Ships as a serving officer. I think that I felt rather strange.

Post-war England was almost worse than wartime England in that shortages of food and everything else seemed to be greater, there was hardly any petrol and England was drab and dull after Australia.

I could have gone up to Cambridge after the war, but I didn't — the Navy had been my University, and for that I shall be eternally grateful.

But my social life had been woefully neglected, I had very few friends, and I decided that if I was going to find a nice girl friend, I had to buy a car, and to buy a car I had to earn some money, and therefore much against my better judgment I agreed with my father that I would go and work in his office.

He told me that my annual salary would be £200, that I would have two weeks' holiday a year, and that I would have every other Saturday off. After six years very varied experience in the Navy, I felt that this transition to civilian life was, on the face of it, very unattractive, but I had to have some money and so I started work. Luckily, despite the low salary, I found that my job was very interesting, and from then onwards I never looked back, but that is another story.